THE [illegible]RY OF HULL'S ORTHODOX SYNAGOGUES

and the people connected with them

ELLIOT OPPEL, M.A., B.Sc., Cert.Educ.

Highgate of Beverley

Highgate Publications (Beverley) Limited
2000

Acknowledgements

In the preparation of this book, I am indebted to the following for their willing help:

The late Jack and Deirdre Lennard for their generous loan of photographs.

The Executive Committee of the Hull Hebrew Synagogue for permission to film both exterior and interior views of the building.

Barrie Donn for his photographic contributions.

Barbara Robinson for typing the original script and many members of Hull's Jewish Community for personal items which they kindly loaned to me.

Front illustration shows eight of the sixteen windows in the Hull Hebrew Synagogue; the remaining eight are on the back cover. Details of their pictorial messages are on pages xi and xii.

British Library Cataloguing in Publication Data.
A catalogue record for this book is available from the British Library.

ISBN 0 948929-16-2

Published by

Highgate of Beverley

Highgate Publications (Beverley) Limited
4 Newbegin, Beverley, HU17 8EG. Telephone (01482) 886017

Printed by

Abbotsgate

4 Newbegin, Beverley, HU17 8EG. Telephone (01482) 886017
Unit 3, Northumberland Avenue, Kingston upon Hull, HU2 0LN. Telephone (01482) 225257

Contents

Illustrations

The Chief Rabbi
Dr. Jonathan Sacks

'We must renew our contribution to British society. Here in this country we love we have found freedom, tolerance and respect for our traditions. Britain was, and is, a moral giant among nations, and we must play our full part in carrying it forward as a caring and compassionate society. As Jews, we should have a principled concern about the environment, about social, medical and business ethics and about the image of G-d in our fellow human being, Jew and non-Jew alike.' – Dr. Jonathan Sacks, Chief Rabbi, Extract from Inaugural address, 1991.

FROM THE AUTHOR

An Apology

It is inevitable, I fear, that a number of personalities connected with the Hull synagogues mentioned, will have been omitted, due to lack of space, or simply insufficient evidence of their official roles during the periods in which they served over the time-span under consideration.

As Samuel Johnson wrote, 'A man will turn over half a library to make "one book",' to which I add, try to forgive the omissions – enjoy the inclusions.

Nevertheless, my apologies are extended to all such persons, both past and present, who should perhaps have been included.

Elliot Oppel

Foreword

Some three centuries, or so, ago, a small Jewish community – probably a mere handful of itinerant salesmen and their families – settled in Hull, and their descendants have, ever since, lived in a city which has shown maximum tolerance and understanding to religious minorities, of which the Jewish immigrants were one.

This is *their* story which, until the opening of the 20th century, saw Hull's Jewish population – never in excess of 2,000 – restricted to the basic accommodation of Hull's Old Town, within the proverbial stone's throw of the Market Place. Familiar street names, like Dagger Lane, Posterngate, Parade Row and Robinson Row, housed the majority of the recently arrived immigrants.

Like all religious congregations, a place of worship – in their case, a Jewish synagogue – was an important, if not *the* most important, part of the community's development and, hopefully, this book lists all such synagogues, from modest buildings holding a few hundred congregants to little more than an individual synagogue member's home.

Historically, the book features Jewish personalities, past and present, set in the context of national and international events that have directly, or indirectly, affected the local Jewish scene.

The earliest arrival of Jewish immigrants to this country in the reign of William the Conqueror; the 'Expulsion' in Edward I's reign (during which Hull was founded); and the 'Return' with Oliver Cromwell's 'blessing' are featured, and locally, we follow the few 18th-century arrivals, to the influx of Jews into the port of Hull from the pogroms of Eastern Europe in the early 1900s.

As a finalé: Jewish education for the young; the opening of Hull's most recent synagogue; and, hopefully not too irrelevant to the main theme, the book features a world-wide look at Jewish personalities as varied as Benjamin Disraeli, David Ben Gurion, Barbra Streisand, Yehudi Menuhin and Anne Frank.

Comment from Councillor P. J. Doyle, M.A., LL.D., D.Litt.

Leader of Kingston upon Hull City Council
(to Elliot Oppel)

I happily respond to your invitation to comment on Hull's Jewish Community, whose valuable contribution to civic life in Hull has been out of all proportion to its numbers.

Among a distinguished list were long-serving Leader of the Council, Sir Leo Schultz; Chairman of the Education Committee, Laurie Science; Chairman of Libraries and Cultural Services, Lionel Rosen; and Louis and Rita Pearlman on the City and County Council respectively. More recently, Philip Bloom was Deputy Leader of the City Council.

The Lord Mayor of Hull readily responds to invitations from synagogues, and chairs the Annual General Meeting of the Hull and District Council of Christians and Jews, at Hull's Guildhall.

The City Council has speedily responded to the Home Secretary's suggestion for a national day to commemorate the Holocaust.

Long may the Hull Jewish contribution to our City continue!

POPULATIONS (Approximate)

Year	*Total Population Kingston upon Hull*	*Jewish Population Great Britain*	*Jewish Population Kingston upon Hull*
1299 Hull's Charter	300 (60 households)	1290 15,000 (approx.) Jews expelled by Edward I. Small number Marranos remained.	
1377	2,000		
1575	4,600		
1643	8,000	1656 Jewish return in Oliver Cromwell's regime.	
1700	7,991	1700 1,000 1734 6,000	
1780	15,000-20,000	1750 8,000	1780 Synagogue Posterngate (5 families) 1796 20-30
1800	27,248	1800 20,000-25,000	1801 31
1851	84,690 C	1850 35,000	1851 67 Census Sabbath
		1875 51,250 (39,835 in London). (1850-1914 peak period	1870 550 1880 600
1901	240,259 C	immigration, 7-fold	1900 1,500-2,000
1911	277,991 C	increase 35,000 to 250,000) 1914 250,000-300,000.	
1951	299,105 C		
1961	303,261	(an estimated	
1971	285,970 C	400,000-450,000 maximum)	
1981	268,300 C		
1991	253,111 C	1990 300,000	
1997	263,900 very approx.		1999 500

C = Census Year.

9-fold increase, in 19th century, due to dock development, improved transport railway and steamships

1960-1997 – Decline in population due to movement out of Hull to more rural districts

In 1990, as shown, the Jewish population of the country was around 300,000, of which 97% were Ashkenazi (people from Central and Eastern Europe) and 3% Sephardi (Spain, Portugal, Holland, Italy etc.) This was from a total national population of 56,370,000, i.e. approx. 0.53%, (1 in 200) Jewish.

An interesting, if not totally significant, statistic gained from the above list is that, at certain periods, the total population of Kingston upon Hull equates approximately to the total Jewish population in great Britain, for example:

Population	*K.U.H.*	*Jewish population G.B.*
1800	27,248	20,000-25,000
1951	299,105	250,000-300,000

Principal Synagogues in Hull from 1780 to present day

(1) 1780 Posterngate (Map 1)
(2) 1809 Parade Row (Map 1)
(3) 1826 Robinson Row (Map 1)
(4) 1878 Nile Street (Map 1)
(5) 1885/1900 Great Thornton Street (Map 2)
(6) 1887 School Street (Map 1)
(7) end c19 Prince Street (Map 1)
(8) 1902 'Hull Western' – Linnaeus Street (Map 2)
(9) 1903 'Hull Old Hebrew' – Osborne Street (Map 1)
(10) 1914 Great Passage Street (Map 1)
(11) 1914 'Central' – Cogan Street (Map 1)
(12) 1928 'New' – Lower Union Street (Map 1)
(13) 1926 Adelaide Street (Map 2)
(14) 1940 West Parade (Map 2)
(15) 1951 Park Street (Map 2)
(16) 1995 'Hull Hebrew Congregation' (see page 28)

Map 1

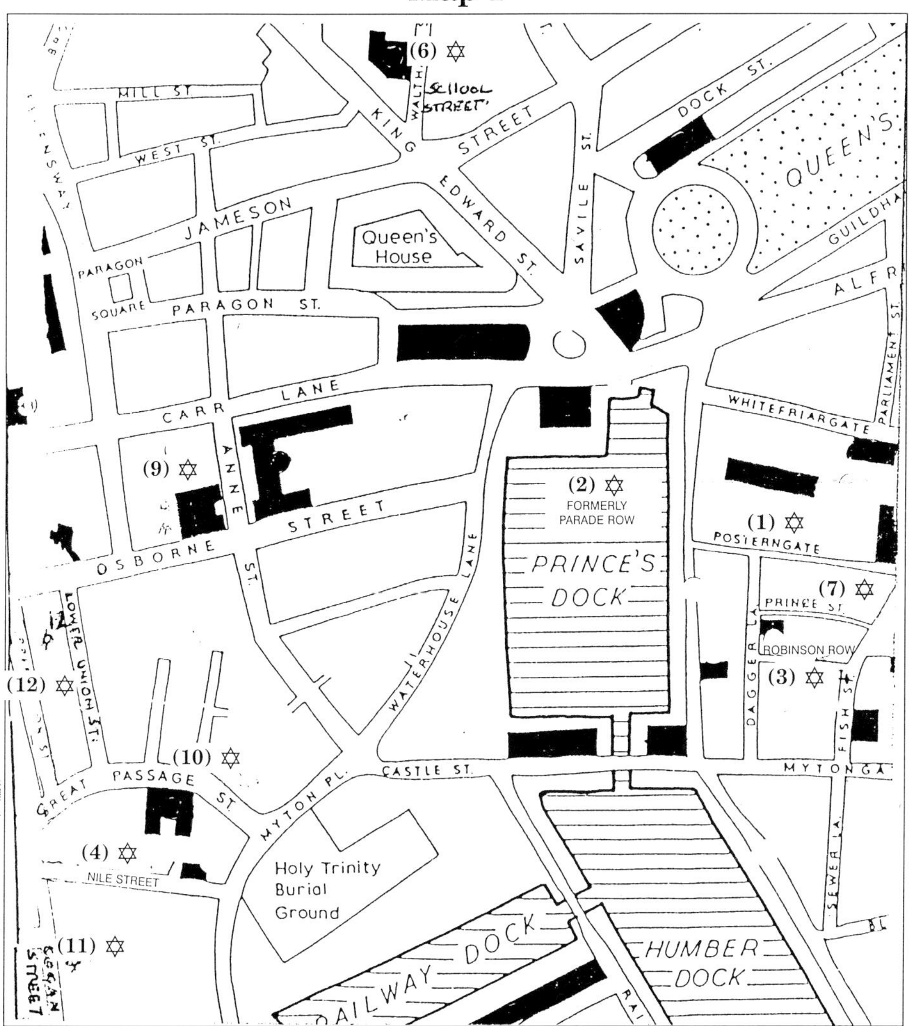

Map 2

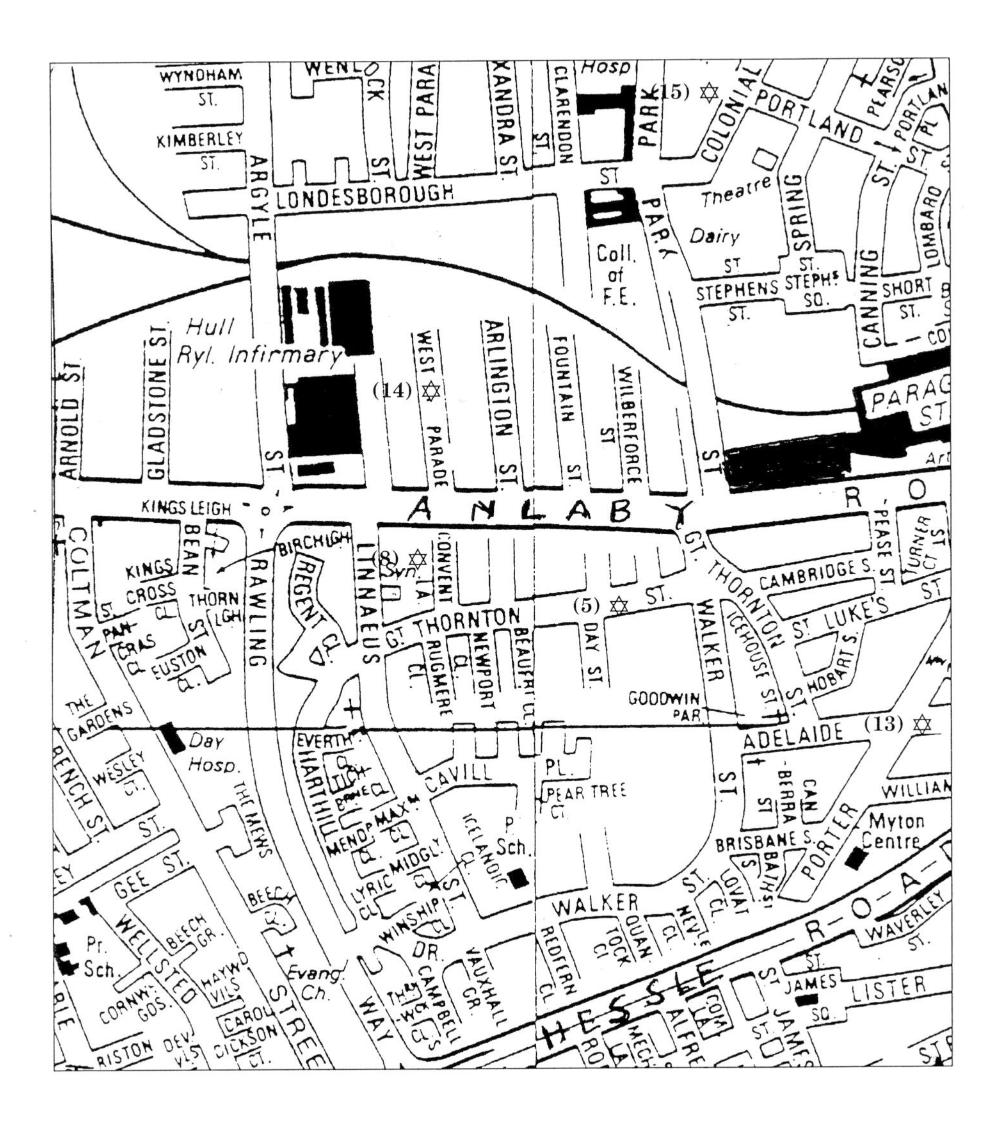

WYNDHAM ST.
KIMBERLEY ST.
ARGYLE ST.
LONDESBOROUGH
WEST PARADE
CLARENDON ST.
PARK ST
COLONIAL
PORTLAND ST.
Theatre
Dairy
SPRING
Coll. of F.E.
STEPHENS ST.
CANNING
SHORT ST.
LOMBARD
Hull Ryl. Infirmary
ARNOLD ST
GLADSTONE ST.
(14)
WEST PARADE
ARLINGTON ST.
FOUNTAIN ST.
WILBERFORCE ST
PARAGON ST
ANLABY RO
KINGS LEIGH
COLTMAN
BIRCHLGH
REGENT CL.
LINNAEUS
(8)
CONVENT LA
GT. THORNTON
(5)
DAY ST.
WALKER ST.
ICEHOUSE ST
CAMBRIDGE S.
PEASE ST
TURNER CT
ST LUKE'S ST
HOBART S.
GOODWIN PAR
ADELAIDE
(13)
RAWLING
RUGMERE CL.
NEWPORT CL.
BEAUFORT CL.
THE GARDENS
Day Hosp.
WESLEY CT.
CAVILL PL.
PEAR TREE CT.
ICELANDIC CL.
P. Sch.
WILLIAM
Myton Centre
PORTER
BRISBANE S.
LOVAT CL.
WALKER
GEE ST.
WELLSTED
BEECH GR.
Pr. Sch.
LYRIC CL.
WINSHIP CL.
CAMPBELL
VAUXHALL GR.
REDFERN CL.
TOCK CL
Evang. Ch.
STREE
WAY
HESSLE
WAVERLEY ST.
JAMES SQ.
LISTER
ST. JAMES

Chronological List of Hull's Orthodox Synagogues

(1780 to present day)

Opening Year of Synagogue	*Location*	*Details*
(1) 1780	**POSTERNGATE** (Off Hull Market Place)	Former Roman Catholic Chapel, sacked by mob (in June 1780) during the Lord George Gordon Riots – continued in use until 1826. Leader of Synagogue: Solomon Meyer. Probably demolished by 1964. Five Jewish families formed initial congregation from a total Hull population of 15,000-20,000.
(2)1809	**PARADE ROW**	On the site which was later incorporated into the Prince's Dock (named in honour of Albert, Prince Consort of Queen Victoria). Founder of Synagogue: Joseph Lyon. 30-40 Jews in Hull's total population of 27,000-28,000 (in 1801).
(3) 1826	**ROBINSON ROW** ('Hull Old Hebrew Congregation')	Combined Posterngate-Parade Row. First foundation stone laid 27 February 1826, by Solomon Meyer (formerly of Posterngate Synagogue). Second foundation stone, on same date, by Israel Jacobs (formerly of Parade Row). Opening ceremony, 18 June, 1827. Virtually re-built and consecrated 26 September 1852. Foundation stone laid by Israel Jacobs. Seating for 200 men and 80 ladies. In 1870 there were 112 members from a Hull Jewish population of around 550. Prime mover of new building was Bethel Jacobs married to Esther Lyon, daughter of Joseph Lyon founder of Parade Row Synagogue.
(4) 1878	**NILE STREET**	
(5) 1885 to 1900	**GREAT THORNTON STREET**	Formerly a mission.
(6) 1887	**SCHOOL STREET** (Central Synagogue)	Used principally by foreign Jews of recent arrival. 90 seat holders. Replaced by Cogan Street in 1914.

(7) end 19th century	**PRINCE STREET**	(Approximately 2,000 Jews in Hull in total).
(8) 1902	**LINNAEUS STREET** (Hull Western Synagogue)	Designed by Benjamin Septimus Jacobs (architect son of Bethel Jacobs) who became its first president. Closed 1994.
(9) 1903	**OSBORNE STREET** ('Hull Old Hebrew Congregation')	Replaced Robinson Row. Enlarged in 1932. Destroyed during air raid in 1941. Re-opened 1955. Closed circa 1993.
(10) 1914	**GREAT PASSAGE STREET**	Formerly a mission.
(11) 1914	**COGAN STREET** ('Central Synagogue')	Replaced School Street. Housed in Salem congregational chapel. Destroyed during the 1939-45 war.
(12) 1928	**LOWER UNION STREET** ('The New Synagogue')	Former Methodist Chapel. Used as a meeting place from 1916; then as a Synagogue from 1928 until 1941. Damaged by bombing in 1939-45 war – repaired – in use by Jewish organisations for some years after, until around 1964.
(13) 1926	**ADELAIDE STREET**	Formerly a mission.
(14) 1940	**WEST PARADE**	Replaced Cogan Street ('Central Synagogue') – probably a large house.
(15) 1951	**PARK STREET** ('Cogan House')	Replaced West Parade – had housed Alderman Cogan's school until 1950. Was originally built as Lister's Hospital. Closed 1976.
(16) 1995	**HULL HEBREW CONGREGATION**	Combined Hull Western and Hull Old Hebrew congregations. Opened 2 April, 1995 (Second Nisan, 5755) by Chief Rabbi Dr. Jonathan Sacks. Orthodox Jewish population in Hull, 450 approximately. The 20th century began with a Hull Jewish population of around 2,000, and enters the 21st century with less than a quarter of that number.

Sources for these dates and figures are numerous and some may prove approximations. However, at least the nucleus for further research by the interested reader is made available.

The windows in the Hull Hebrew Synagogue with Biblical verses explaining their various messages

PEACE WINDOW

'O Lord and King of Peace, who created all things, help all of us, that we may forever adhere to the concept of true and abundant peace, prevailing between man and man, and between husband and wife, so that no strife separates mankind even in thought.
Extend your heavenly peace to us and to the whole world, so that all discords be resolved in great love, and all shall come near to you and form one union to do your will with a whole heart.
O Lord of Peace, bless us.'

Nachman of Bretslav

CREATION

'In the beginning G-d created the heaven and the earth. Now the earth was unformed and void, and darkness was upon the face of the deep; and the spirit of G-d hovered over the face of the waters.'

Genesis 1: verses 1-3
Soncino Chumash

STREAMS ON DRY GROUND

'I thank Thee, O Lord, because Thou has put me
at a source of flowing streams in dry ground,
a spring of water in a land of drought
channels watering a garden of delight,
a place of cedar and acacia;
together with pine for Thy glory,
trees of life in a fount of mystery,
hidden amid all trees that drink water.
They shall put forth a branch for an eternal planting;
taking root before they sprout.
They shall send out their roots to the stream;
its stump shall be exposed to the living water,
and it shall become an eternal source.'

From *The Language of Faith* by Nahum N. Glatzer.

THE TREE OF LIFE

'It is a Tree of Life to those who grasp it,
and those who support it are fortunate.
Its ways are ways of pleasantness
and all its paths are peace.'

Proverbs 3: verse 17.

THE BURNING BUSH

'And the angel of the Lord appeared unto him, in a flame of fire out of the midst of the bush; and he looked, and, behold, the bush burned with fire and the bush was not consumed.'

Exodus 3: verse 2

JACOB'S LADDER

'And Jacob went out from Beersheba and went toward Haran, and he lighted upon a certain place, and tarried there all night, because the sun was set; and he took some of the stones of that place, and put them for his pillows, and lay down in that place to sleep. And he dreamed, and behold a ladder set up on the Earth, and the top of it reached to heaven and behold the angels of G-d ascending and descending on it.
And behold, the Lord stood above it, and said, "I am the Lord G-d of Abraham thy Father, and the G-d of Isaac: The land whereon thou liest, to thee will I give it, and thy seed." '

Genesis 28, verses 10-13

THE TALLIT WINDOW

And the Lord spake unto Moses saying: 'Speak unto the children of Israel, and bid them that they make them throughout their generations fringes on the corners of their garments, and that they put with the fringe of each corner a thread of blue. And it shall be unto you for a fringe, that ye may look upon it, and remember all the commandments of the Lord, and do them.'

Numbers Ch.15, verses 37-39, Soncino 'Hertz' Chumash.

THE SABBATH WINDOW

'The three Mitzvot, Mikvah, Challah and lighting the Shabbat candles.'
'Grace is illusive and beauty is vain, but a woman who fears the Lord – she will be praised.'

From Aishes Chayil, Proverbs 31: verse 30

THE PARTING OF THE SEA OF REEDS

'And Moses stretched out his hand over the sea; and the Lord caused the sea to go back by a strong East wind all the night, and made the sea dry land and the waters were divided. And the children of Israel went into the midst of the sea upon the dry ground; and the waters were a wall unto them on their right hand, and on their left.' Exodus, Ch.14, verses 21-22.

'And Israel saw the great work which the Lord did upon the Egyptians, and the people feared the Lord; and they believed in the Lord, and in his servant Moses.'
Verse 31. From the Soncino Chumash.

THE SACRIFICIAL FLAMES

'The fire offerings of Israel and their prayer accept with love and favour, and may the service of your people always be favourable to you.' Shemoneh Esrei (Art Scroll Siddur)

'And the priest shall make it smoke upon the altar, upon the word that is upon the fire; it is a burnt offering, an offering made by fire of a sweet savour unto the Lord.'
Leviticus 1, verse 17. Soncino Chumash.

THE BLESSING OF THE NEW MOON

'Blessed is He whose utterance created skies,
The breath of his lips all of their host.
Law and time he fixed for them
That they alter not their function.

Joyous to do the will of their Master,
True labourer, whose labour is truth.

And the moon, He bade renew,
Garland of glory for those borne from the belly,
Destined like her to renew
And to glorify their Maker
For the honour of His kingdom.

Blessed art Thou, O Lord,
Who renews the moons.'
From *Language of Faith*
by Nahum N. Glatzer. Sanhedrin 42a.

On back cover

CHARITY HARVEST

'The following are the commandments as to which no measure is imposed; leaving the corner of the field, offering the first fruits, gifts on appearing at the Sanctuary on the three festivals, charity and the study of the Law.' From the Morning Service.

THE SHOFAR WINDOW

'Speak unto the children of Israel saying, "In the seventh month, on the first day of the month, shall be a solemn rest unto you, a memorial proclaimed with the blast of horns, a holy convocation".'
Leviticus 23, verse 23.

'And in the seventh month, on the first day of the month, ye shall have a holy convocation: ye shall do no manner of servile work; it is a day of blowing the horn unto you.' Numbers 29, verse 1.

THE MEMORIAL WINDOW FOR THE SIX MILLION

'Who knows, it might even be our religion,
from which the world and all peoples learn
good, and for that reason and that reason
only do we have to suffer now!' Anne Frank.
- died in Bergen-Belsen Concentration Camp, March 1945, at 16 years of age.

DANCE (KING DAVID'S DANCE)

'Praise Him with tambourine and dance;
Praise Him with strings and pipe.' Psalm 150, verse 4.

MUSIC

'Praise Him with trumpet sound;
Praise Him with lute and harp.' Psalm 150, verse 3.

Introduction

Anyone seeking written material regarding the history of Hull's Orthodox Synagogues – over a near 300-year span – would be presented with a verbal *cul-de-sac*, as such material is difficult to come by. This book, which accompanies my Video[1] on the same subject, is a modest attempt to fill the yawning religious gap. My overall aim is to look at Hull's Orthodox Synagogues in the context of the history of the Jewish peoples, at local, national and international levels.

Some historians will claim that Jewish entry into this country, and hence their accompanying Houses of Prayer, can be traced back to Roman times, but it was truly only at the time of the Norman Conquest of England that a settled Jewish community began.

William, Duke of Normandy – William the Conqueror – who reigned from 1066 to 1087, attracted a Jewish following at the time of his activities at the Battle of Hastings. The Jewish immigrants had assumed (as will be seen later, quite wrongly) that England was a land flowing with biblical milk and honey, a safe haven for its immigrant Jewish population. The truth was very different, effectively summarised by the 13th-century monarch, Henry III, as follows:

> 'All Jews, wherever in the Realm they are, must be under the King's protection, nor can any of them put himself under the protection of any powerful person without the King's licence, because the Jews themselves, and all their chattels, are the King's . . . If anyone detain them or their money, the King may claim them, if he so desire, as his own.'

Jewish life in England in the 12th and 13th centuries was – as in other periods of Jewish

Statue of King Edward the First – Founder of Kingston upon Hull, 1299 – stands in the foyer of Hull's Guildhall.

House in Lincoln, traditionally known as 'Jews' House'.

history – dominated by anti-Semitic riots and the imposition of harsh taxes against the religious minority unwilling to convert to Christianity as the Church would have them do.

Mob attacks on the Jewish communities, such as those in Norwich and London, climaxed in the tragedy at Clifford's Tower in York in 1190, when many Jews committed suicide to avoid falling into their intended captors' hands. This typified the terror under which the Jewish population of this country lived. The cathedral city of Lincoln still has signs of a 12th-13th century Jewish presence. A Norman house lived in by Jews of the time still exists. The Lincoln Jewish community, after a century or more of persecution, fled the City, a handful returning in recent years.

Henry III's eldest son, Edward I, at the time of his succession to the English throne in 1272, was taking part in the Crusades. On his return to England in 1274, he was faced with an impoverished Jewish community who were accused of usury;[2] 'clipping the coinage' to allegedly produce more coins; and even such shameful accusations as ritual murder were made. Hence there existed a disillusioned Jewish community, whose leaders pleaded with the King to 'Let my people go!'

And go they did!

On 18 July, 1290, corresponding to the ninth day of the Jewish month of Av, the Decree of Expulsion was signed by Edward.

Either by a startling coincidence[3] or by deliberate design by Edward, the date was the anniversary of the destruction of the two Temples in Jerusalem, the first in 586 B.C.E. by the Babylonians, the second in 70 C.E.[4] by the Romans.

The 9th day of the Jewish month of Av, commemorates the destruction of both the first and second Temples in Jerusalem, in 586 B.C.E. and 70 C.E. respectively

On Tuesday, 10 October, 1290, the Exodus of the Jewish population of this country began – perhaps around 15,000[5] – the first-ever banishment of Jews from a European country. Any Jew still on English soil on 1 November, 1290, was liable to the death penalty. Their ultimate destinations, in the main, were France and Spain. The anticipated massacres of Jews did not occur, although individual cases of cruelty were reported. Basically, the Expulsion went apparently smoothly.

Within a decade of the Expulsion, the same monarch, Edward I, had founded Kingston upon Hull and granted its Royal Charter in 1299. The year 1999 saw Hull celebrate the 700th anniversary of the receipt of its Royal Charter, the contrast between the fates of' Jews and non-Jews being seen to have been startlingly different some seven centuries ago.

'From now on,' states the Charter, 'the men of Hull are free and can leave their house and land to anyone they want.' Such freedom was a far cry from the rampant anti-Semitism nationwide, which had created the conditions for the Expulsion from these shores of' the Jewish minority for in excess of three and a half centuries.

Although the Jews were not re-admitted to this country until Oliver Cromwell's day, there was always a small but continuous Jewish presence during the Expulsion years. The so-called Marranos[6] lived allegedly as 'converts' to Christianity while practising Judaism in secret; others hid their religious roots as well as possible from the authorities, risking life and limb in the process.

Oliver Cromwell, who took a pro-Jewish stance to the return of the expelled Jews to this country.

The principal resettlement of Jews in this country dates from 1656, and two totally differing leading figures, a Dutch Rabbi and the Lord Protector, Oliver Cromwell, were central to what many would agree was one of the most important dates in Anglo-Jewish history.

The first of the duet was, by name Rabbi Manasseh Ben Israel, a Marrano and a powerful man of religion in Amsterdam, who pleaded with Cromwell to allow Jewish re-entry to this country. His 'Humble Address', dated November 1655, began:

> 'To His Highness the Lord Protector of the Commonwealth of England, Scotland and Ireland. The Humble Address of Manasseh Ben Israel, a Divine and Doctor of Physick, on behalf of the Jewish Nation.'

On 4 December, 1655, a Conference, with Cromwell at its head, met in Whitehall to discuss whether it was lawful to re-admit the Jews, since their Expulsion in 1290 had never been by Act of Parliament simply a Royal Decree of Edward I, binding only during Edward's reign. Ironically, based on this pronouncement, the Jews might have returned legally at any time after Edward's death in 1307. Leading lawyers declared that there was no law which decreed that the Jews could not return to England. In spite of opposition from the clergy and tradesmen (in fear of competition from a flourishing Jewish banking and merchant class) Cromwell took the view that the Jews would provide a variety of new trades to improve the economy after the Civil War. Taking a distinctly pro-Jewish stance, Cromwell was probably the first national leader to take such a kindly approach to a Jewish minority which then – and since – showed total loyalty to the countries in which they were allowed to live in peaceful fashion. Some

Rabbi Manasseh Ben Israel who, with Oliver Cromwell's 'blessing', was the architect of Jewish resettlement in Britain.

historians will argue to this day about Cromwell's motives, be they political, humanitarian or economic. It is most assuredly simplistic to reason in 'black and white' terms. He was a man of his time, whose complex character varied from the bravery and responsibility of a war leader to a firm religious belief in the imminent Second Coming of *his* Messiah.

English ecclesiastics were also of the opinion that Christ himself would appear when all Jews embraced the Christian faith, and this was more likely to occur if the Jews returned to this country, the *only* country in which a Jewish presence did not exist.

There specially existed a distinct empathy between Manasseh Ben Israel and the Puritans in England, who had a common love and respect for the Old Testament. Manasseh Ben Israel also sought *his* people's Messiah and concluded that a Jewish presence in *every* country on earth was vital to that end. He returned to Holland in 1657 a disappointed man, since the edict he sought for Jewish re-admission to this country had not been formally granted. Nevertheless, a growing sympathy towards the Jewish cause undeniably existed. Within two months of his return, Manasseh Ben Israel had died at a mere 53 years of age, probably unaware of his great claim to fame. The influx of Jews to Britain was proof enough that, even though their motives were different, the unusual duet of Manasseh Ben Israel and Oliver Cromwell had succeeded in their mutual aims.

Oliver Cromwell, the 'Jewish Champion', died in September 1658. Cromwell's reign was briefly taken over by his third son, Richard, who abdicated in May 1659. The Monarchy was restored in May 1660, with Charles II (1660-1685), son of the beheaded Charles I, on the throne.

In 1664, a Privy Council ruling stated that the Jewish presence was officially accepted, 'so long as they (the Jews) demean themselves peaceably and quietly, with due obedience to His Majesty's laws'. Fear still persisted that the passing of Oliver Cromwell would bring with it a return of the former State interference with the religious way of life of the Jews, but, with few restrictions, the general acceptance of the Jews to practise their faith became a gradual, and hardly noticeable, process.

In 1673, the religious status of British Jews was legalised in writing – the first time that that had occurred! Charles II, whose queen, Catherine of Braganza, had employed a Jewish physician, Fernando Mendez, was very appreciative of the financial help given to him by the Amsterdam Jewish community. This resulted in a royal show of goodwill and a continuation of State protection of the Jews, which tended to defuse any anti-Jewish behaviour which still existed. The last of the Stuart kings, James II (1685-1688) created freedom of religion for the Jews, dampening down growing anti-semitism with the edict, 'They (the Jews) should quietly enjoy their Religion'.

Successive British monarchs appreciated all too well the ability of their Jewish population to 'enrich' the country, not purely in a financial manner, but with a wealth of ideas in the worlds of economics, medicine and the arts.

The English throne was successively occupied by William III (1689-1702) and Mary II (1689-1694); Anne (1702-1714);[7] George I (1714-1727) and George II (1727-1760), during which, if a Jewish presence existed in Hull at all, it would in all probability have been made up of a handful of itinerant pedlars.

Hull's Jewish Synagogue Beginnings

'A small community can still be a great community.'

Chief Rabbi, 2nd April, 1995 (Hull).

When the Hull Town fortifications were levelled in 1774, Jewish human remains were found just inside the walls. In addition, several Jewish artefacts, including tephilin (tiny boxes interlaced with leather strings, used during morning prayers and containing parchment inscribed in Hebrew with passages from Exodus and Deuteronomy) were also discovered. All the human remains faced towards the East – a Jewish burial custom – hence an early Jewish cemetery apparently existed in the area together, presumably, with its attendant synagogue.

Detailed statistics of the period are difficult to come by, and even more difficult to prove, but a Synagogue in Dagger Lane – originally named 'Ten Faith Lane' – apparently existed during the 17th century, only to be demolished around 1700.

In a work entitled *An Ancient Synagogue in Hull*, John Symons states that the Synagogue was 'on the west side of Dagger Lane, about half way down . . . The gateway opened from Dagger Lane into a courtyard, and then took its course to the end, nigh to the town walls, where the said Synagogue stood. It was built in the Tetra style. It was of such beauty, all adorned with stone pillars, covered with flowers of the most grand description. The pulpit was of polished oak and stood on four pillars, fluted, the first being ornamented with gold mouldings and pictures of Abraham, Isaac, Jacob, David and Solomon. The fronts of the women's balcony were filled in with words taken from the Talmud. . . (Jewish oral law, which generations later was committed to writing). Around the year 1700, the place was getting into a decayed state, so it was pulled down, and was found to be built on arches, the walls being four feet thick and formed of hewn stone.'

It was some 20 years into the reign of George III (1760-1820) that Kingston

Roman Catholic Chapel, destroyed in Gordon riots. Rebuilt as Synagogue, in Posterngate, in 1780.

upon Hull celebrated the opening of its first Synagogue, of which more substantive evidence is available.

Around five or six immigrant families – approximately 20 men, women and children, from a total Hull population of around 15,000-20,000 – had sought out a property in Posterngate,[8] off the Market Place, in Hull's Old Town. The Synagogue leader was Solomon Meyer. The building was a former Roman Catholic chapel, ruined in the riots of 1780, when the somewhat eccentric Lord George Gordon, who had been a vociferous defender of the Protestant faith, led the anti-Popery riots. They came about when Catholic Irish labourers arrived in England and took the jobs which the indigenous population maintained they had a right to and were prepared to use violence in their cause.[9] To add a touch of irony to the scene, Lord George Gordon was later received into the Jewish faith, taking the Hebrew name Israel Ben Abraham, only to die in 1788 in Newgate Prison. His incarceration was, somewhat incomprehensibly, as a result of having uttered a libel against Marie Antoinette, Queen of France. The sacked Posterngate property was re-built and presumably it could maintain a regular minyan.[10]

It is fair to assume that one of its congregants was Michael Levy, a watchmaker, who was the first Jew to live in Hull, in the year 1770. The Posterngate Synagogue continued to operate until 1826.

Meanwhile, some 17 years earlier, in 1809, a second Hull Synagogue had been opened on a site in Parade Row, later incorporated into the Prince's Dock (named in honour of Albert, Prince Consort to Queen Victoria). The founder of the Synagogue was Joseph Lyon, who, apparently due to disagreements

Unique photograph of now defunct Robinson Row Synagogue showing its semi-circular windows

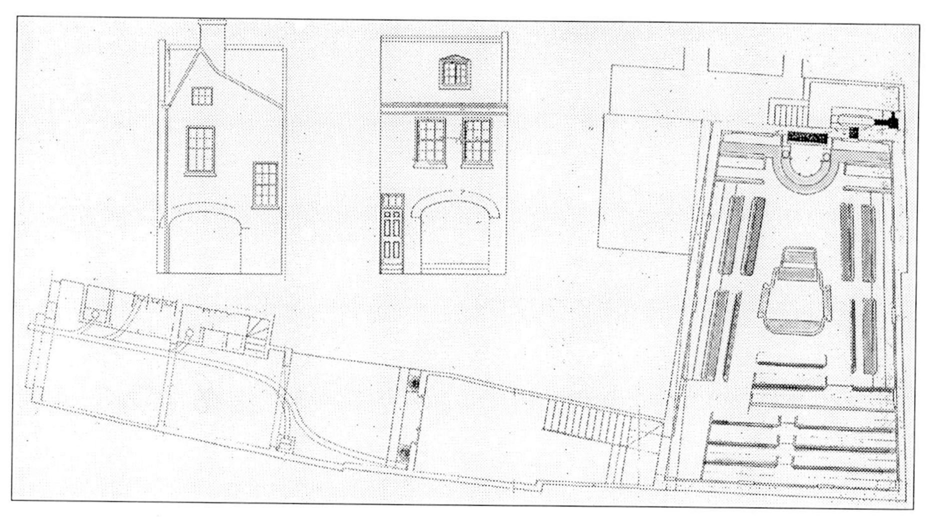

Ground plan of Robinson Row Synagogue.

HULL.

HULL HEBREW CONGREGATION.
SYNAGOGUE (1874)

Robinson Row.

Has seat accommodation for 210 persons: 120 gentlemen's seats; 90 ladies' seats. Seat Rental—from £1 6s. ro £7 10s. per annum.

Secretary—Isaac Hart, 9, Ocean place.

HONORARY OFFICERS.

President—Solomon Cohen, 67, Queen street.
Treasurer—Aaron Feldman, 46, Saville street.
Committee—Marcus Casril, 10, Tynemouth street.
Hyman Gerson, 84, Porter street.
Victor Glasman, 72, Lister street.
Abraham Goodman, 14, John street
Max Maguer, Lister street.
Lewis Marks, Waterworks street.
Marcus Markwald, Fish street.
Aaron Shoolberg, 115, Porter street.
John Symons, 72, Queen street.
Shochet, Mohel, and Second Reader—Rev. David Rosenthal, Blackfriar gate.
Beadle— Manheim, Trundle street.

HULL HEBREW SCHOOLS.

West Street.

BOYS' SCHOOL

Hebrew Master— Greenberg, Porter street.
English Master—I. Dalton, Mason street.

GIRLS' SCHOOL

Mistress—Miss Jones.

President—Mrs. Bethel Jacobs, Beverley road.
Hon. Secretary—Mrs. Solomon Cohen, 67, Queen street.
Hon. Teachers—Miss Jacobs, Beverley road.
Miss Moseley, Whitefriar gate.

JEWISH SOUP KITCHEN.

Lower Union Street.
Founded 1872.

Object—To provide food on Sabbaths and Holydays to poor Jews arriving from Continental ports.

President—Israel Goldman, Brook street.
Hon. Secretary—Abraham Hiller, Groat Passage street.

with the officials of the Posterngate Synagogue, decided to 'go it alone'. (Hull's synagogue history shows that these differences of opinion among congregations and their leaders tend to follow a relatively common formula, as will be seen during the last quarter of the 20th century).

However, in 1826, there was a meeting of minds; the old wounds of controversy were healed and Posterngate and Parade Row amalgamated in nearby Robinson Row. The Minister, Samuel Simon, who had combined his ministerial salary at Parade Row, with a probably more lucrative income as a seller of spectacles, now became a full-time minister in the new building. Hence the 'Hull Old Hebrew Congregation' was re-born with foundation stones being laid by Solomon Meyer (a pawnbroker) of Posterngate, and Israel Jacobs (a jeweller) of Parade Row, on 27 February, 1826. The opening ceremony was on 18 June, 1827.

The Robinson Row interior was described in this fashion: (See diagram page 3).

> 'Interiorly it is a neat apartment, lighted from the top, having a gallery along three of its sides for the female portion of the congregation. On the floor, in the centre of the building, is a raised platform, in front of which is a reading desk. This platform is called the behmah, or reader's desk.
>
> At the East end, on a dais, beneath a handsome portico supported by Corinthian pillars, is a kind of safe or Tabernacle, called the 'Holy Ark', in which are deposited the Scrolls of the Law, the Five Books of Moses . . .
>
> Above the Ark is a semicircular window filled with stained glass, and one of the compartments represents the two Tables of Stone, having the Decalogue inscribed thereon in Hebrew characters.
>
> In front of the Ark hangs the perpetual lamp.'

The Robinson Row Synagogue was to become the centre of Jewish life in Hull for a quarter of a century. A religious census, dated 30 March, 1851, showed that 74 congregants attended morning services, 17 in the afternoon and 21 in the evening, with 95 services in all each year.

A virtual re-building of the Synagogue a year later, in 1852, provided seating for 200 men and 80 ladies, around double the initial 1826 accommodation. The foundation stone was laid by Israel Jacobs, whose son, Bethel (1812-1869) was the predominant Jewish figure of the period. The enlarged Synagogue allowed for a more egalitarian approach for its members, as cheap – and even free – seats were introduced for the less well-off. By 1870 membership rose to 110 from a Hull Jewish population of around 550.

Bethel Jacobs was the prime mover, both in terms of raising finance and in the general supervision of the 'new' Robinson Row building. Among his host of offices were: Town Councillor; President of the Hull Literary and Philosophical Society; and President of the Mechanics Institute, and he was also a lecturer and vocalist! On his death, on 26 December, 1869, the *Hull News* used the phrase, 'A Jew true to his faith', as the ultimate tribute to his memory.

The Jacobs' family name (with Benjamin Septimus and Joseph Lyon to come) continued to be highly respected in both Jewish and non-Jewish circles.

A further lay leader, who formed an outstanding duet with Bethel Jacobs, was George Alexander, who, like Bethel Jacobs himself, was of the 'Anglicised' tradition, and was allegedly the earliest Jew to be *born* in Hull (in 1791). He was a well-known silversmith and jeweller, and served as President of the Synagogue on several occasions. He died in 1865, at the age of 75.

Robinson Row's continuation for much of the remainder of the 19th century was in the face of growing difficulties, due to lack of space for an increasing community, allied to growing friction between the emotional European Jews, and the more placid Anglicised members of the congregation. Social status also played its part as the attraction of the palatial properties (at the time) of Beverley Road and Anlaby Road – especially Coltman Street – created a Jewish exodus from Hull's Old Town and, in consequence, a desire for a more accessible House of Prayer.

There also existed an in-built hierarchical system in the Synagogue, in which Mid-European Jews regarded themselves as superior to their Russian counterparts, and the original settlers, namely the English, felt superior to both, even though they were less likely to be regular Synagogue attenders.

Meanwhile, Jewish persecution had reached savage proportions in both Russia and Poland, and, like their biblical ancestors who fled from the Egyptian Pharaoh, the Exodus began, with its consequent effect on the Jewish population of Great Britain in general, and Hull in particular.

As history shows, the policy of some governments, when faced with public discontent, caused by unemployment and poor living standards, is to lay blame on their vulnerable religious minorities. A virulent anti-Semitic campaign resulted in Eastern Europe, with its Jewish population – although suffering the same privations as the vast majority – being singled out for verbal and physical abuse, which, not unnaturally, led to their Exodus to the West.

The Press headlines had screamed their terrifying messages:

'Peasant slaughters entire Jewish family'.
'Jews terrorised in Russia as shops and homes are sacked.'
'Massacres in Tsarist Russia'.
'Plea to dying Tsar to show compassion.'

It all led to a wave of Jewish emigration, with Britain as the first port of call, since ships re-fuelled at British ports, Hull, being (next to London) probably the most significant, receiving some 300-400 immigrants annually. It was not so much a pre-determined decision by the immigrants to seek a specific country, more a determination to leave behind them the horrors of Eastern Europe – an escape-route! Some travelled on to Leeds, Liverpool and the U.S.A. Others, of course, stayed in Hull, producing a crying need for additional Synagogue accommodation.

The Jewish population of this country escalated seven-fold (35,000 to 250,000) from 1850 to 1914, the coming of the railways being a vital factor in the accelerated flow of Jewish immigration. However, long and difficult rail and sea journeys were no guarantee of a good life to come for the impoverished immigrants on their arrival in this country.

So-called, 'professional' employment was denied the Jewish immigrants, who had little, if any, knowledge of the English language, speaking, in the main, Yiddish.[11] A common sight was to see Jewish pedlars, with packs of merchandise strapped to their backs, providing the needs of countryside dwellers in an age when shops were principally found in towns. These itinerant salesmen were probably members of some synagogue in London, which had the nation's largest Jewish population by far in Great Britain, and, of course, still has.

What employment did exist for the Jews was principally found in the tailoring industry, a magnet for Jewish commercial life. Alec Levine's workshop in Pease Street, Hull, provided a typical example of a demanding job in which long hours and cramped conditions were the norm.

The massive problem of poverty among the 600 or so Hull Jews in 1880 was partially alleviated by the formation of the Hull Hebrew Board of Guardians. The Robinson Row Synagogue Council had met on 12 November of that year in the vestry in the Synagogue itself to declare formally the birth of the Movement.

Under the initial presidency of Joseph Lyon Jacobs (1838-1883), the first of ten children from the union of Bethel Jacobs (a leading, Hull solicitor) and Esther Lyon, the Board assisted 'more than one-third of the Hull Jewish population', who were 'in a state of dire poverty, and this at a time when the immigrants were coming in large numbers'. (From *A Short History to Commemorate the Centenary Year*, by Sydney Burnley, the Board's President.)

The Hull Hebrew Board of Guardians, under its present title, 'Hull Jewish Community Care', over a century later (albeit with the residents enjoying a far better standard of living than their 19th-century predecessors), are now housed in a fully-equipped and recently enhanced property on Hull's Anlaby Road, a mere stone's throw from the previously-mentioned Coltman Street, the *crème-de-la-crème* of the earlier Jewish settlers.

Alec Levine's workshop in Pease Street, Hull.

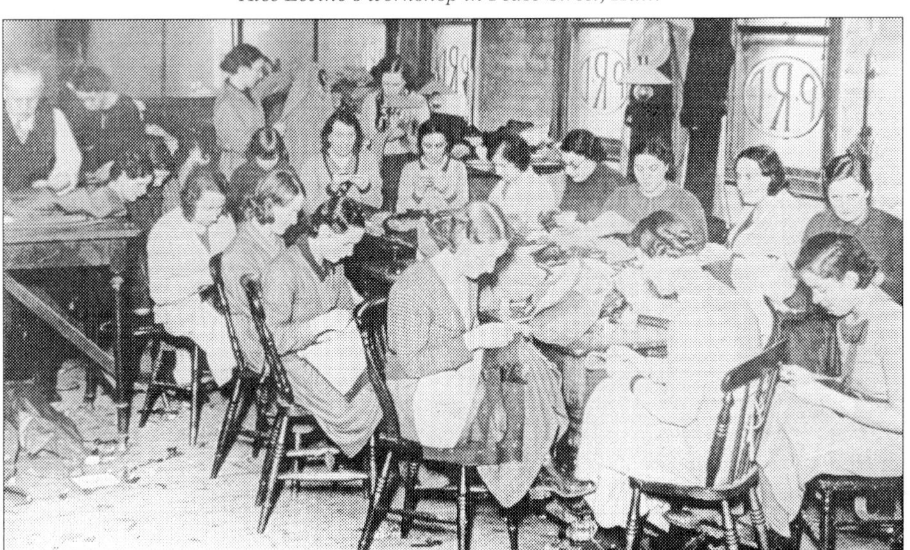

The human stories behind some who chose Hull as their home

Hilda and Solomon Oppel

One of the many thousands who escaped from the Russian pogroms [12] was my own father, **Solomon Oppel**. He had been sent to England by his parents as a child, for his safety. He served in what was then Palestine with the British Army in the 1914-1918 War, and eventually married my late mother, **Hilda**, who was born in Hull. Solomon became a commercial traveller, a natural continuation of the pedlars of an earlier generation, and Hilda was a self-employed dressmaker, working from our less-than-modest home in Hull's Old Town.

Jack Lennard, a well-known Hull entrepreneur, took a keen interest in the influx of Jews from the Russian area. His father had appealed directly to the Kremlin in Moscow to release the oppressed Jewish population who wished to emigrate, and Jack, as Chairman of the Wilberforce Council,[13] continued his mercy-missions, travelling to Russia several times.

Dr. Solomon Lurie, a former President of the Hull Western Synagogue (see Page 41) for 25 years, and son of a Rabbinical scholar, Rabbi Jacob David Lurie, came with his family to Hull from Bialystock, in Eastern Poland, as a child. He served the Hull community as a member of the medical profession for 50 years, having qualified in 1938, as well as holding office in a number of Jewish organisations, including the presidency of the Communal Talmud Torah and Chairman of the Hull Jewish Representative Council.

Among current regular Synagogue attenders is **Benno Eisner**. Born in Vienna in 1924, Benno, as a 15-year-old, was sent by Kindertransport to England to escape the Nazi threat, arriving merely a week before the outbreak of the 1939-45 War, His father, Joseph, of whom he has not heard since, had been sent to Buchenwald concentration camp; his mother, Regina (who, until

Jack Lennard with efigy of William Wilberforce.

her recent death, was in constant contact with Benno), had travelled to the U.S.A.

Benno, an active member of Hull Association of Jewish Ex-Service Men and Women, is their proud standard-bearer. His Army service was spent in the Pioneer Corps, which he joined, aged 20, five years after his arrival in England. Being a 'Cohen', namely a descendant of the priests of Ancient Israel, Benno has the unique privilege of being 'called up' first, to recite a blessing during the Synagogue Torah readings.

Eastern Europe was not the only area from which Hull's Jews escaped the horrors of anti-Semitism. Egypt can be added to the list, with the unsympathetic King Farouk as its leader. **Maurice Sultan**, together with his parents and eleven brothers and sisters, left their home in Heliopolis, a suburb of Cairo, as late as the year 1950, their travels taking them to France, Mexico, Israel and England. A recently retired businessman, Maurice, with his wife, Barbara, happily settled in Hull and are justifiably proud of the youngest brother in Maurice's family, David Sultan, who, ironically, became Israel's ambassador in Egypt before transferring to a similar post in Canada.

The only Hull Jewish man to suffer the appalling brutality of a Japanese Prisoner-of-War camp, for an interminable period of 3½ years, is former Western Synagogue, now Pryme Street, congregant, **Leslie Kersh**.

Now in his mid-eighties, but looking at least 20 years younger, Leslie had been liberated from Changi Jail, Singapore, suffering from the deficiency disease, beri-beri. He was reduced to a skeletal 6½ stones, little more than half his normal weight. Called up in 1940, Leslie had trained as an anti-tank gunner at Catterick, was promoted to bombardier (Royal Artillery), and transferred overseas, to end up in Singapore after serving in Sierra Leone, West Africa, Bombay and Columbo. The surrender of the Japanese forces by Emperor Hirohito, in August 1945, signalled Leslie's 'demob'. This is an astonishing story of a local hero who modestly summarises his experiences with the words, 'Will-power alone saw me through'.

One of the first, if not *the* first, Military Cross to be awarded to a soldier of the East Yorkshire Regiment in the 1939-45 campaign, went to Western Synagogue member, the late **Major 'Billy' Sugarman**. Billy was at the initial landings of British Forces at Normandy, in June 1944, and was twice wounded. At a later stage in his Army career, he fought in the Eastern campaign in Burma. On Billy's return to civilian life he became a Hull headmaster.

A further unique human story with a strong religious connection concerns retired Hull G.P., **Dr. Carl Rosen** and his three Cambridge graduate sons. The Rosen family – members of both the 'Old Hebrew' Synagogue and the 'Hull Western' maintain the truly Orthodox tradition of Judaism. Eldest son, Jonathan is now a Rabbi in Jerusalem, editing a variety of religious publications, a far cry from his earlier entry into the legal profession as a member of the Middle Temple, in London. Consultant cardiologist, Stuart, works in a London hospital, but is never too far away from his religious roots as a lay Synagogue official, often conducting services. Carl's youngest son, Joseph, like his eldest brother, is a Rabbi, also in Jerusalem, with Torah study and teaching as his forte.

Those of us who live our entire lives in one city will raise an eyebrow at the lifestyle of a retired Hull doctor's son-in-law whose travels took him from his birthplace in Morocco to Binyamina in Northern Israel and then, by marriage, to Hull.

Hull Hebrew Synagogue member **Joseph (Yossi) Casslasy** (son in law of Dr. Louis Jaffe) has been in Hull for 14 years, with wife Diane. Their son Daniel is a 6th form student.

Yossi's war was fought, not in the 1939-45 campaign on the battlefields of Western Europe, but as a paratrooper in the Israeli Defence Forces during the Yom Kippur (Day of Atonement) War, of 1973, when, on 6 October, Syrian tanks attacked Israeli positions in the Golan Heights, the natural northern mountainous defensive border between the two countries, (this was, of course, in addition to the Egyptian attacks in the Sinai). Within 3 days the Golan Heights were re-taken by the Israeli Army and, with both American and Russian political influence, the war – which had threatened World Peace – became a stalemate, ending some 17 days after it began.

Yossi spent a total of 3½ years fighting for his Country's freedom, as did his three brothers. His parents are still in Binyamina, which Yossi continually proclaims as Israel's true 'capital'. (Binyamina is named after Baron Edmond de Rothschild – his Hebrew name being Binyamin. A great philanthropist towards the Israeli cause be became the first Honorary President of the Jewish Agency. The remains of Edmond, and his wife Adelaide, lie in the Rothschild gardens in Zikron Yaacov, a few miles from Binyamina). Yossi's father was employed as a gardener in the beautiful surroundings for most of his life in Israel.

These are, of course, only a few examples of the many hundreds of Jewish residents who had sought refuge and peace of mind in Hull, a City which has always proved a great friend to its Jewish community.

In spite of the insuperable difficulties which the Jewish immigrants faced, their living conditions in England were undeniably a great improvement compared with their past experiences. Provincial Jewish communities in this country came into existence throughout the middle and second half of the 18th century, not surprisingly, seaports tending to dominate, e.g. Hull.

The period 1837-1847 seems to have marked the 'birth' of provincial Anglo-Jewry in general, with varying numbers, from a mere 65 in Hull to the combined communities of Birmingham, Liverpool and Manchester providing 50 per cent of the provincial total of around 7,000 to 8,000. Next in line came Brighton, Bristol, Canterbury, Chatham, Edinburgh, Glasgow, Plymouth, Portsmouth and Swansea, with between 100 and 300. The remaining towns had fewer than 100 in their Jewish communities.

The rural Jewish pedlar was 'transforming' into a shop-keeper; the young Jewish boy had taken up an apprenticeship; and slowly but significantly, the 'respectable' jobs previously denied them became available.

As the 20th century opened, Hull's Jewish population had swelled to the 1,500 to 2,000 mark, its highest ever!

The Hull Western Synagogue

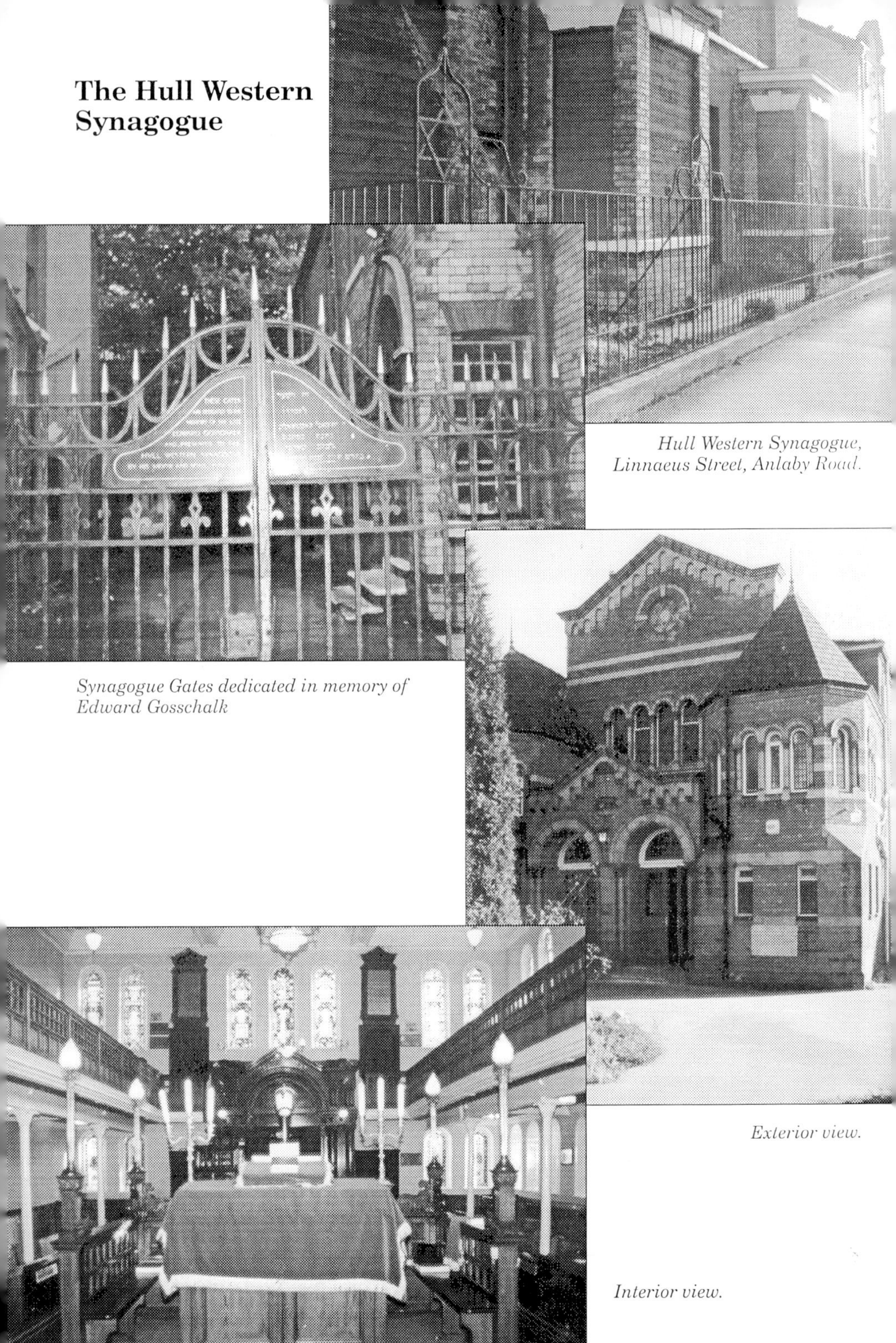

Hull Western Synagogue, Linnaeus Street, Anlaby Road.

Synagogue Gates dedicated in memory of Edward Gosschalk

Exterior view.

Interior view.

The Hull Western Synagogue

'It is a long drive (from London to Hull) but since I kept seeing the signs which said "Services 35 miles", I knew that I was on the right road for a Shool (Synagogue).'

– Chief Rabbi, 2 April, 1995 (Hull).

Just two years into the 20th century, when Hull's Anlaby Road trembled to the sounds of the tramcar, the Hull Western Synagogue was born in Linnaeus Street.[14] As mentioned earlier, lack of space at Robinson Row and the attraction of better housing were the dominant factors which decided the move, and a Synagogue close at hand became a vital need, since Orthodox Jews, according to Jewish law, are compelled to walk to and from the Synagogue on the Sabbath and Festivals.

Mr. B. S. Jacobs.

The 'Western's' first President, who served in that position for the first 25 years of the Synagogue's existence, was Benjamin Septimus Jacobs (1851-1931). He was the 10th child of the union between Bethel Jacobs and Esther Lyon, daughter of Joseph Lyon of the Parade Row Synagogue. An architect of considerable repute, B. S. Jacobs[15] designed and arranged the building of the 'Hull Western' and its adjacent school.

H. Feldman, J.P., C.C.

A powerful duet of principal members of the Synagogue consisted of B. S. Jacobs himself and his Vice-President, Henry Feldman, J.P., who was elected as the first Jewish Mayor and Chief Magistrate[16] of Hull, occupying the position for four successive years from 1906 to 1909 (see Page 40).

Henry Feldman was a well-known woollen merchant who lived in Linnaeus Street, opposite the newly-constructed Synagogue. His all-round linguistic ability in Hebrew, French and German, allied to his Talmudic artistry, resulted in the Synagogue Council placing on record his 'rare gifts of heart and command' on his death in March 1915. Henry was the product of a family immersed in the Jewish tradition. His father, Aaron Feldman, was a man deeply involved in the congregational life of the city, and Aaron's wife, Rachel Harris, was the daughter of Nathan Harris, known as 'Reb Nachum', the 'father' of Talmudic study.

The Synagogue's gates were dedicated to the memory of Edward Gosschalk, the foundation stone being laid on 25 September, 1902, by Osmond Elim D'Avigdor Goldsmid, who was later knighted. The Reverend Harris Cohen was elected as first Cantor in June 1902, to be replaced by the Reverend H. Alperovitz, who stayed until the outbreak of the First World War in 1914. Harry Goldberg was the first barmitzvah boy in the new Synagogue.

In the Synagogue's early years, the contrast between the rather emotional European element of the congregation, many of whom spoke mostly Yiddish, and the 'English gentlemen', of which B. S. Jacobs was one, demanded considerable tact by the Synagogue's leaders to keep matters on an even keel; but, as the years passed, more disciplined behaviour gradually appeared.

Considerations of space and time make it inevitable that only a small number of 'Western' personalities can be considered, beginning with the special name of Cantor Joshua Freedberg, appointed in July 1926. He was a man with a deep love of the Torah,[17] who, in addition to leading the Synagogue services, gave tremendous energy and devotion to forming, and training a male choir which sang for the Sabbath and Festival services, many of the tunes being Cantor Freedberg's 'originals'. Principal chorister in the Reverend Freedberg's choir for many years was Judah Rose, who quite obviously regarded the task as a true labour of love, and whose deep, sonorous voice is still to be heard, being a regular synagogue attender and former Warden.

Cantor Joshua Freedberg.

A contemporary of the Reverend Freedberg was the Reverend David Hirsch, B.A., a powerful presence in the pulpit when in full verbal flow. He held office from 1931 to his death in 1950. Reverend David Hirsch, in an emotional plea for the creation of a Jewish State, continued the inspirational example set by his father, Rabbi Dr. S. A. Hirsch, who was a leading figure in the Choveve Zion(Lovers of Zion) who unobtrusively founded some of the original settlements in Palestine such as Rishon-le-Zion (started with the help of the Rothschild family, in 1882) and Rosh Pinah in the Galilee, founded in 1879.

Reverend David Hirsch

The Reverend Hyman Davies (affectionately known as 'Hymie'), who arrived in Hull in 1948, devoted virtually his entire career to the 'Western'. In earlier days (March 1920) came Rabbi L. Miller, who officiated at my late parents' wedding, and who later moved to Middlesbrough, and, in 1953, came Rabbi E. S. Rabinowitz, B.A., a highly impressive and equally talented community leader. The name Broder proved prominent at the 'Hull Western' when Rabbi Irvin Broder saw two of his three sons follow in father's footsteps into the clergy – the third joining the teaching profession. Son Gavin became Chief Rabbi of Ireland and Rabbi

The Reverend Hyman and Mrs. Davies.

Rabbi E. S. Rabinowitz, B.A.

Irvin himself took over one of the, if not the, largest Jewish community in London, namely Ilford. Emeritus Rabbi Dr. Chaim J. Cooper, M.A., Ph.D. served the community for some four decades until his sad demise in late December 1999.

Mr. H. Harris had been elected Beadle from the outset, having become the Synagogue's first salaried official. A three-year tenancy of the position was held by Mr. J. Brown from late 1916 to the appointment of his successor, Morris Abrahamson, who held the position for 24 years, from just after the ending of the 1914-18 War until his death in August 1943. Morris's means of transport was a bicycle! His son, Abe – well known over the years as a Hull accountant and one of the Hull Judeans' leading table-tennis players (see page 47) – relates how his eldest sister, Annie, after her father's death, took over his administrative responsibilities until the appointment of the legendary Harry Westerman in November 1944.

'Harry', as he was known to one and all, was much more than a fee-collector. He carried out a host of other duties, including possibly the most important of all, that of making funeral arrangements,[18] including the ritual washing of the body – the 'Taharah' – a duty of respect and kindness from the community to the deceased.

Above all, Harry was a personality with a warm sense of humour, and a commitment to the Jewish community over a 54-year span. Although principally employed by the 'Western', Harry's religious boundaries were limitless, regardless of the individual's 'affiliation' to one Synagogue or another. Harry died in January 1998, a truly sad loss felt by everyone. There is obviously something very special about the role of Shammas.[19] which lives on long, long after their earthly duties cease.

The 'Western's' Presidential chair was occupied from 1944 to 1970 by Dr. Solomon Lurie. An impressive plaque is prominently displayed to the side of the Holy Ark in the new Synagogue to record Dr. Lurie's long-term service. Dr. Lurie and the aforementioned B. S. Jacobs in total served for more than half the Western Synagogue's lifetime (see list of Presidents, page 41).

Dr. Solomon Lurie.

For the final fifteen years of Dr. Lurie's twenty-five year 'reign' as President of the 'Western', his colleague as Vice-President, Louis Harris, had seemingly little in common with the Synagogue leader.

While the good doctor tended the sick, businessman Louis (in his younger days, of course) dashed down the wing at Craven Park, the home of Hull Kingston Rovers Rugby League team. The somewhat rare sight, namely a *Jewish* Rugby League professional, Louis played for Hull K.R. from 1919 to 1929, and then turned his energies to the Board Room as a director. He won two Championship Medals and was awarded an M.B.E. for his sterling work for the great War Trust, an organisation formed to assist World War One victims.

These contrasting figures as Synagogue President and Vice-president, apparently worked with great effect, since they became (together with the B. S. Jacobs/H. Feldman duo), the longest-serving Synagogue top officials in the 90 year 'Western history.

Incidentally, Louis Harris's father as mentioned earlier, was, 'Hull Western's' first shammas.

One congregrant who has the unique honour of having held all four Executive positions – Secretary, Treasurer, Vice-President and President – also served as Warden of the most recently-built Pryme Street synagogue is Conrad Segelman, who, from 1958 to the present day, has taken a continuous role in the affairs of the Synagogue.

The Hull Western's President's Board has a distinct grandfather-father-son look about it when it comes to the name Rosenston. Harry Rosenston was the 'Western's' third President from 1929 to 1941, following B. S. Jacobs (1901 to 1926) and B. Franks (1926 to 1929). Harry's grandson, Norman, was President from 1970 to 1975, and he was succeeded, more than a decade later, by Norman's son, Cyril, from 1987 to 1991 (see list of Presidents on page 41). Cyril's father-in-law Emmanuel (Manny) Marks, was a prominent lay official and President from 1980 to 1983, and a Warden in the new Synagogue, but tragically died within 18 months of the Synagogue's formal opening in April 1995.

A short walk from the 'Western' brought you to the Hull city centre, its Market Place, and Hull's theatre-land where the Grand Theatre presented a variety of entertainment; both amusing and serious. The Tivoli Theatre provides fond memories to this very day, for those of us who've left behind our 21st birthdays some years ago. Household names such as Wilson, Keppel and Betty, with their highly original sand-dancing routine; 'Old Mother Riley', played by Arthur Lucan, who died during a performance at the Tivoli, in 1954, and whose grave is situated in the East Hull cemetery; and the 'Jewish Pavarotti' of' his day, Issy Bonn, who insisted on stating that he 'didn't want to set the world on f-i-r-e', he just wanted to 'start a flame in your heart'. Desperately old hat possibly, compared with our modern musical age but it nevertheless combined good family comedy and singing, with a hint of nostalgia.

The fashion world was dominated by Emily Clapham, better known as 'Madame Clapham', Hull dressmaker extraordinaire, who in her heyday in the Victorian and Edwardian eras, had an international clientèle, successfully competing with the leading fashion houses of Paris and London. She founded work-rooms at No.1, Kingston Square, Hull, in 1887. Madame Clapham died in 1952, at 96 years of age.

Issy Bonn.

'Old Mother Riley' – Arthur Lucan.

Retracing our path to the 'Western', the middle period of its existence was dominated by War, when, like other major Synagogues in Hull, it suffered incendiary bomb damage early in the 1939-45 conflict. Nevertheless, services were held on a daily basis and the Synagogue Council's maintenance programme saw to it that the postwar building showed few signs of damage. The 'Western's' survival after the War was in stark contrast to the tragic destruction of the 'Old Hebrew' and the 'Central', as will be seen later.

The 'Western's' closure came in 1994, after a decade of murmurings, and sometimes downright hostility, due to varying opinions expressed by the members of the Synagogue regarding the 'Western's' future. To parody the Bard, 'To close or not to close' was the on-going cry!

The call for the Synagogue's continuation, with all its attendant fond memories of parents, grandparents and other relatives, had vainly tried to take precedence over the more cold, practical considerations of ever-increasing maintenance costs, borne by the ever-decreasing Hull Jewish Community.

The cold facts won the day, as they always do, and a 'thing of true beauty' in its heyday has for some years past stood as a lonely, desolate building, calculated to depress those of us whose thoughts of the old 'Western' are tinged with happy – and sometimes quite sad – memories.

Left: The Grand Opera House.

Below Left: 'Madame' Clapham.

Below right: The Tivoli Theatre.

Hull Old Hebrew Congregation

Hull Old Hebrew Synagogue –
View from Anne Street.

Hull Old Hebrew Synagogue Ark.

Menorah
(eight-branched candlestick).

Hull Old Hebrew Synagogue – View from Osborne Street.

The Hull Old Hebrew Congregation

'Our strength has never lain in numbers – less than one per cent in the world. The entire population of the entire Jewish world is equivalent to the statistical error in the Chinese census.'

Chief Rabbi – 2 April, 1995

A few months after the 'Western' came into being, a new Synagogue, 'The Old Hebrew Congregation', opened in what, at the time, was Hull's main street of Judaism, Osborne Street, the Jewish population in Hull being around 2,000.

During the lifetime of the Synagogue, Jewish traders' names and occupations had a familiar ring about them: Hyman Freedman, the baker; Abraham Sugar and Sons, suit materials and accessories; Ben Marks's grocery store, with its strong aroma of smoked salmon and pickled gherkins; Koppel Peysner, the butcher; Pinchas Hart, the draper; Jack Levine, the fishmonger – a veritable Old Time Jewish 'Tesco', set in the one small centrally-placed Hull street, a street which provided most of the Old Hebrew Synagogue's congregation.

The 25th September, 1902, must have proved to be a busy day for Osmond D'Avigdor Goldsmid, for his duties had included both the foundation ceremony for the 'Old Hebrew' and the aforementioned 'Hull Western Synagogue'.

The Hull 'Old Hebrew' was opened on 10 September, 1903, by Albert Holt of London, who had previously lived in Hull, and Rabbi Professor Hermann Gollancz, (who was at the time Minister of Bayswater Synagogue in London), consecrated the building, the service being conducted by the Reverend H. Bendas, assisted by a choir. The Royal Prayer proclaimed the blessing for 'Our Sovereign Lord King Edward (VII), Our Gracious Queen Alexandra, and all the Royal Family'

Within the first few years of the 'Old Hebrew's' existence, financial troubles occurred, as in 1912, when the Minister, the Reverend H. Bendas, sought some £600 to clear an outstanding mortgage repayment, of which £400 had been offered, with some £200 still to find. 'We are compelled,' he wrote, 'to appeal to the philanthropists of Anglo-Jewry'. That £200 figure must seem a pittance in this day and age!

On 17 July, 1932, there was opened on the same site an extensively re-built and much enlarged Synagogue with a Beth Hamedrash.[20] The consecration was by the Chief Rabbi, Dr. Joseph Herman Hertz, the Synagogue being re-opened by Alderman Benno Pearlman, who rose to the prominent position of Lord Mayor of Hull. Isaac Levy laid the foundation stone. Accommodation was available for 700 congregants with a further 140 in the Beth Hamedrash.

Less than 10 years later, on the night of 7-8 May 1941, severe bombing from German air raids in the 1939-45 war resulted in the destruction of the Synagogue[21], the Beth Hamedrash thankfully surviving, although badly damaged. Four years passed, almost to the day, when the headline, 'War in Europe is Over', greeted us on 8 May, 1945!

On the world scene, 14 May, 1948, saw the State of Israel come into being, under its first Prime Minister, David Ben Gurion. In 1952, King George VI died, and so did Israel's first President, Chaim Weizmann. A year later (1953) H.M. Queen Elizabeth II was crowned in Westminster Abbey and Edmund

Hillary and Sherpa Tensing conquered Mount Everest (29,002 ft.) for the first time. In 1955 brilliant scientist Albert Einstein died, and 1 September that year saw the Hull 'Old Hebrew' Synagogue's re-birth on the same site as its predecessor.

Rabbi Dr. Myer Lew, Dyan of the London Beth Din, who consecrated the Synagogue, accorded unstinting praise to the Cromwell era in his speech at Hull's City Hall. Such an eminent Jewish leader must surely have silenced Cromwell's critics with these words, 'We are always profoundly and sincerely mindful that, since the wise statesmanship of the Protectorate of Cromwell opened the gates of this hospitable land to our persecuted and wandering brethren, Jews in this country have gained slowly an emancipation and equality which has enabled so many to play their part worthily in the political, industrial and economic life of this country. It was a wise and humane statesmanship and we are proud to acknowledge it publicly.'

The Synagogue was re-opened by its President, Louis Rapstone, an outstanding Jewish figure of the period, who had served as both Treasurer and President for many years (see page 42). His retirement years were spent in Israel. A plaque to recognise his achievements stated: 'To mark his untiring efforts during the period of World War II, during which this Synagogue was destroyed by enemy aircraft. His leadership preserved this congregation and later directed it through the various stages of its reconstruction until the work was completed.' The foundation stone had been laid some months earlier by Mr. A. Levine.

Risking the venom resulting from any omissions from the 'Old Hebrew' honours list, let us begin with the clergy. Initially, Rev. Dr. Salis Daiches (1903-1906) and the aforementioned Rev. H. M. Bendas led the newly formed Osborne Street Synagogue Community.

Synagogue President Louis Rapstone and wife Peggy; Mrs. Regina Bentley and husband Harold (Treasurer).

Rev. A. Warshawsky with Executive and Council, at his installation in 1927.

From just after World War I – about 1919 – the triple responsibility of Chasan, Shochet (authorised slaughterer of animals according to strict kosher requirements) and Mohel (circumcises male Jewish infants, eight days after birth), was held by Reverend Harry Abrahams. Harry was born in Palestine around the turn of the century, married a Grimsby girl, and had served in Bolton and Broughton (Manchester), before taking the Hull appointment; (his son, Leslie, is a highly respected Warden of the present Hull's Pryme Street Synagogue). After leaving Hull, Reverend Abrahams went to Stockport, but returned to Hull in due course to assist the Park Street Synagogue.

Successive clergy included: Reverend Warshawsky (1927-31), Reverend Krushevski (1933-39), long-serving Reverend J. Levinson (1932-1956), Reverend Willencyk (1957-1973), Reverend Caplan (1973-1978) and Rabbi Dr. C. J. Cooper until the Synagogue's eventual closure.

Rev. J. Levinson.

The Synagogue's early years produces memories of Rabbi Samuel M. Brod. A publication of Rabbi Brod, dated 1931, and printed in Poland, has surprising connections with the Hull Old Hebrew Synagogue.

Rabbi Brod's daughter was the grandmother of Barbara Brody (née Johnson), whose mother and father, Gertie and Archie Winer, lived in Hull throughout their lives, with Archie acting as Shool Shammas at the 'Old Hebrew'.

Barbara, now living in Lytham, brings Lancashire and Yorkshire Jewry close together as she writes with great affection of Rabbi Brod, her great-grandfather.

A necessarily limited random selection of personalities of the 'Old Hebrew's' days gone by include: J. E. Cohen's 'pious dedication as President over many difficult years during and after the First World War'; Jack Levy, 'an Honorary Officer of distinction at the time of the expansion of 1932'; Phineas Hart, 'an active Honorary Secretary whose orthodoxy and sense of duty were proverbial. His services on behalf of Jewish immigrants should not be forgotten'; Barnett Goldstone 'Secretary for 25 years from 1920 to 1945'; David Robinson, 'who, as an Honorary Officer during the trying years of the 1939-45 War, and beyond, has not lived to see the fruition of the labours to which he contributed so much'. Louis Rosenblum 'who enlivened the congregation by his bonhommie and loyal efficiency'; and Louis (Leib) Finestein, Synagogue Secretary from 1948 to 1956, who penned the above quotes in the souvenir brochure of September 1955, when the Synagogue's reconstruction occurred – and to whom I express my gratitude for the preceding details.

Other long-serving officers were: Henry Taylor, Treasurer (1962-1980) and H. M. Bentley, who served as President from 1958 to 1975, with a short break in 1964. Uniquely, the Synagogue's last President, from 1987 to its closure, was Barrie Donn, M.A., who had earlier (1975-1987) served as Secretary (see page 42).

The distinction of serving in all four executive roles was held by Harry Schulman, Secretary, Vice-President and President from 1964 to 1986, and then, after a seven-year gap, Treasurer until the Synagogue's closure.[22] Harry was, in March 1994, made the third Honorary Life President of the 'Old Hebrew', following in the illustrious footsteps of Louis Rapstone and Henry Taylor.

An interesting tail-piece occurred a few months after the Synagogue's closure, when two sealed time-capsules were uncovered during the Synagogue's demolition. They contained a copy of the *Eastern Morning News* dated Thursday, 25 September, 1902, together with two pre-decimal one-penny coins of the same year.

Max Gold, a Synagogue Committee member at the time, expressed astonishment at the excellent condition of the 'finds' Max having warned the contractors of the possibility of such a discovery.

More than 90 years had passed since the 'Old Hebrew' had opened, and now, due to falling numbers, it had closed! Therefore, just one Hull Orthodox Synagogue – the 'Western', which itself would suffer the same fate within a year or so, remained.

Hull's civic leaders decreed a 'modernisation' of the City centre and, by so doing, swept away all signs of the dwellings of the immigrant Jewry of years gone by. Hull's 'centre' of Judaism had gone forever.

On 31 December, 1993, the final service took place at the 'Old Hebrew', Harry Schulman turned the key in the door for the last time and he and his co-religionists swelled the 'Hull Western' ranks one day later, the opening day of 1994.

Buildings come and buildings go, but pleasant, or depressing, memories live on throughout one's life, and the memories of the 'Old Hebrew' fall principally into the former category.

The Central Synagogue

'We (the Jewish people) have a history which is three quarters of human civilisation, the first to see G-d in history.'

Chief Rabbi, 2nd April, 1995 (Hull).

In addition to the two major-sized Hull synagogues, there was apparently a need for a third in School Street, off Waltham Street, opened in 1887 and replaced in 1914 by a building in Cogan Street, formerly known as the Salem Congregational Chapel. Not surprisingly, due to its location, the Synagogue became known as the 'Central'.

Principally used by immigrant Jews, the 'Central' was opened by Chief Rabbi Joseph Hertz, accompanied by Mendel Marks and Lazer Specterovski. Its first President was Jacob Marks, who was presented with the 'key of the door' on 10 September, 1914, a year which heralded in World War I.

Opening ceremony, 'The Central' l to r Mendel Marks, Chief Rabbi Joseph Hertz, Laser Specterovski. (1914).

'The Central' on site of Salem Congregational Chapel, Cogan Street.

An extract from a publication entitled *Subjects of an Elevating and Sacred Character*, by E. Eberson, dedicated to the 'Central Hull Hebrew Congregation', gives a clear indication of the financial plight of the early Jewish congregation who worshipped there. To quote:

> 'There are but few of the community in question what may be termed well-to-do, and this, being one of the nearest ports to the Continent, there is a continual stream of influx of poor people who are in immediate want of relief, such indeed being the case, the outside world cannot possibly conceive the great strain upon their resources for charitable purposes. The above described pressure having become so apparent that a considerable portion of the poorer classes were determined to provide themselves with a public place of Worship and Burial Ground; and now unfortunately their financial strength being entirely exhausted, they have no other alternative but to commit their present position to the public in general, with the following appeal . . .'

The sale of the publication, at one shilling each (five pence in modern currency), apparently assisted to 'liquidate a considerable debt'. A turn of phrase indicative of its time (early 20th century) sees the author apologising for his 'feeble endeavours', not being 'a native of this country', but conscientiously claiming to have been accompanied by 'sincerity and devotion' in his literary efforts.

Fate was to add to the financial distress a yet greater concern. The 1939-45 World War saw the 'Central's' demise when it (like the 'Old Hebrew'), was destroyed in one of Hull's many severe air raids.

A building (probably a large house) in West Parade replaced the 'Central' in 1940, and was itself replaced in 1951 by what had been the Alderman Cogan School, opposite what was then the Hull Children's Hospital. The location was Park Street, which then, as now, ran from the familiar Anlaby Road to Spring Bank, another of Hull's main arterial roads.

Memories of Park Street go hand in hand with memories of a former generation of 'Frummers' – very orthodox Jews – such as Sam Mostyn (whom I was privileged to work under when he was Deputy Head of Hull's Wilberforce High School on Leicester Street, Beverley Road), and the Hart family, including Max, who taught at Newland High School, Hull, congregants of total orthodoxy who set an inspirational example to the Hull Jewish community in general.

Among the early leaders of the Synagogue were: Jack Marks, Issy Appleson and Boris Furman, but little more than a generation later, due, presumably, to falling numbers (about 80 congregants), the Park Street President, the late Maurice Lipman,[23] and Vice-President, Dr. Louis Jaffe, had to accept a practical approach to their religious futures.

Nostalgia and sentiment for the 'good old days' were, regretfully left behind and a mini-exodus in the direction of the 'Hull Western' on Linnaeus Street resulted.

Hence, Park Street Synagogue was sadly no more.

Other Hull Synagogues

'Rabbi Akiva, some 1900 years ago, was asked by a Roman lady, "You believe that the Almighty created the Universe in seven days; what has He done since?" Rabbi Akiva replied, "He sits and arranges marriages".'

Chief Rabbi, 2nd April, 1995 (Hull).

Now long-forgotten were synagogues in Great Passage Street (1914); Adelaide Street (1926); and Lower Union Street, which was opened in 1928 by Lord Rothschild and named 'The New Hebrew Congregation'. The founder was J. Fischhoff.

The 1950s saw the celebration of the Tercentenary of the Jewish Resettlement in this country. The Duke of Edinburgh, Prince Philip, in a speech in London's Guildhall in June, 1956, summed up the 300 years of the Jewish contribution with the words: 'The Jewish community's record in this country is truly remarkable. Every part of our national life has been enriched by your contribution over the years'. Prime Minister Anthony Eden paid this tribute: 'Let us freely acknowledge that they (the Jews) have richly repaid their welcome here.'

Opening of 'New Hebrew Congregation' – 9 September 1928 – Synagogue founder, J. Fischhoff. (6th from right).

The Years of Attrition

'I shall bring you to the land about which I raised My hand to give it to Abraham, Isaac, and Jacob, and I shall give it to you as a heritage . . .'

Book of Exodus

Map of Israel

'This law (The In-Gathering of the Exiles) declares that the State does not confer on any Jew outside the right to settle in Israel; the right is inherent in his very Jewishness: it is his to exercise at his own free will.'

David Ben Gurion (1886-1973), Israel's first Prime Minister

In the three decades which preceded the creation of Hull's new Synagogue (in April 1995) events in that melting pot called the Middle East came with dramatic regularity.

Since the birth of Israel on 14 May, 1948,[24] the first half-century of its existence had experienced successive periods of war and peace. The security of a small and vulnerable country had always been its basic aim, an aim continually punctuated by the noise and smell of conflict:

1967, 5 June: The Six-Day War: Egypt's President Nasser had threatened Israel with a Muslim Holy War. The Israeli Air Force launched a pre-emptive attack, destroying the aerial capabilities of the Arab States. The brilliantly successful campaign was planned by the then Minister of Defence, Moshe Dayan. It proved to be a war in which the principal centres of power, the USA and Russia, had kept to the sidelines. 338 Israelis and more than 12,000 Egyptians lost their lives in the conflict.

1972, 5 Sept: Arab terrorists murdered 11 Israeli athletes at the Olympic Games in Munich, Germany.

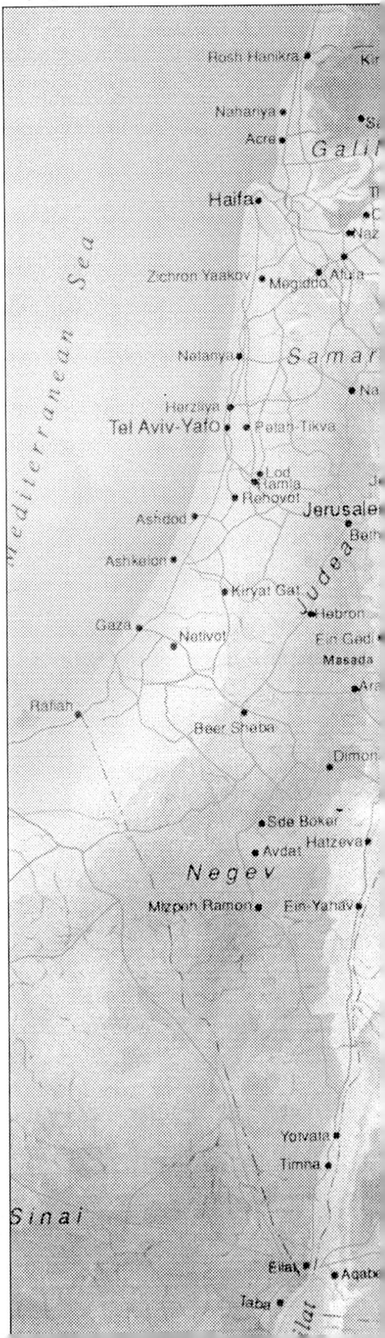

1973, 6 Oct: The armies of Egypt and Syria launched a surprise attack on Israel, the Yom Kippur War. A peace treaty with Egypt resulted – 1,700 Israeli deaths.

1977, 19 Nov: The world was stunned when Anwar Sadat, President of Egypt, arrived in Israel to initiate a peace process.

1978, 18 Sept: U.S. President Jimmy Carter, Israeli Prime Minister Menachem Begin and Anwar Sadat met at Camp David. On 26 March, 1979, a peace treaty between Israel and Egypt was formally signed. Tragically, Anwar Sadat's undeniable bravery cost him his life by assassination.
Sinai peninsular occupied in 1978, returned to Egypt in 1979.

1991: Gulf War – Israel attacked by Saddam Hussein of Iraq.

1992: Israel and Palestine Liberation Organisation (P.L.O.) agreed to establish Palestinian self-rule in Gaza Strip and Jericho in occupied West Bank.

Moshe Dayan and Yitzhak Rabin enter the Old City of Jerusalem.

1994: Israel-Jordan peace treaty signed.

1995 4 Nov: Assassination of Israeli Prime Minister Yitzhak Rabin (1922-1995) by Yigal Amir, a Jewish extremist, ironically after a Peace Rally in Tel Aviv. Rabin's funeral was attended by leading world figures including U.S.A.'s President Clinton, Jordan's King Hussein, Egypt's President Mubarak, Prince Charles, British Prime Minister John Major, and representatives from many Arab countries with which Israel, at the time, had no formal diplomatic relations. A memorial service at London's Royal Albert Hall was attended by more than 8,000 people. Such world-wide grief was (in the light of political events current at the time) both somewhat surprising and equally heart-warming to the Jewish nation. Nevertheless, an allegedly extremely religious Jew not only broke a fundamental commandment but also threatened the Nation's future by the assassination of the Head of Government. Violence of Jew against Jew was, and is, a totally unacceptable concept for both Israeli Jews and, indeed, Jews world-wide, regardless of any alleged provocation.

Yitzhak Rabin's grand-daughter, Noa Ben Artzi, in an understandably emotional few words, effectively proved how her grandfather had appealed to the Jews of former generations

and equally to the young immigrants with the words:
'People greater than I have already eulogised you, but none of them was fortunate like myself to feel the caress of your warm, soft hands, and the warm embrace that was just for us, or your half smiles that will always say so much; the same smile that is no more, and froze with you.
I have no feelings of revenge because my pain and my loss are so big, too big . . .'
Yitzhak Rabin followed the life pattern of several Israeli army leaders, eventually transferring from soldier to politician.

Born in Jerusalem of American immigrant parents, he became a professional soldier, seeing action in successive military campaigns: firstly, the 1948 War of independence when Israel was invaded by the combined armies of Egypt, Jordan, Iraq, Syria and Lebanon; secondly the 1956 Sinai-Suez War. In 1964, he attained the ultimate accolade of Chief of Staff of the Israeli Army. It was his superlative military strategy together with the genius of Moshe Dayan, that brought victory for the vastly outnumbered Israeli Army in the Six-Day War of 1967.

At the beginning of 1968 Rabin left the army to take a major political appointment as Israel's Ambassador to the United States of America, a post he held for five years.

On his return to Israel, he became Prime Minister following the resignation of Golda Meir, in 1974. He tended his resignation three years later, but returned to lead his country for the second time as prime Minister (and Minister of Defence) in July 1992 before his tragic assassination some three and a half years later.

Yitzhak Rabin's successor was Shimon Peres who was narrowly defeated by Benjamin Netanyahu in the election of 1996.

1999, 7 Feb: Death of King Hussein of' Jordan, due to cancer. Eldest son, Abdullah, becomes king.

1999, 17 May: Israel elections – Labour landslide! Benjamin Netanyahu's three-year reign, as Prime Minister, came to an end. Netanyahu also relinquished his leadership of the Likud Party. Labour leader Ehud Barak was overwhelmingly approved as Israel's Prime Minister by the Knesset (Parliament) on 6 July, 1999.

As this book goes to print, Israel is celebrating its 52nd anniversary of Statehood, a State that has paid a high human price of around 19,000 soldiers who have died fighting for its survival. In addition, 77,000 have been disabled – in total approximately 2 per cent of Israel's 4.76 million Jews – based on figures from the Central Bureau of Statistics, which quotes 4.76 million Jews from a 6-million population.

War has been a continual fact of life for the Israeli people, from carnage on the battle-field to carnage on the streets of Jerusalem.

And so to the Present

'I believe in the sun even when it is not shining.
I believe in love when I cannot feel it.
I believe in G-d even when He is silent.'

Written by Jewish Holocaust victims on the walls in Cologne

With the 'Western' being the only Orthodox Synagogue still in existence in Hull, history repeated itself.

Just as the Robinson Row Congregation had clamoured for a new Synagogue in a better class district, so, as a result of a majority decision at a Special General Meeting held on 2 May, 1993, at the 'Western Synagogue', and after a decade or more of argument and counter-argument, the decision was made to pool all available monies and move to Pryme Street, Anlaby, thereby converting an old defunct factory into a brand-new Synagogue. A minority of congregants – including myself – had felt that the unique beauty of the 'Hull Western' could never be recaptured, and that a maintenance programme would ensure its future for at least 50 years, a view which the architect present at the Special General Meeting unreservedly accepted. But the groundswell of opinion demanded, and got, a Synagogue in an area in which the majority of the Jewish community lived.

The generosity of a Hull Jewish schoolmaster, John Woolfe (who had taught myself the rudiments of English in my sensitive teenage years at Hull's Kingston High School), proved the deciding factor when a significant shortfall in finance existed. Mr. Woolfe's legacy to the 'Hull Western', of which he had been a member, created the financial foundation for Hull's new Synagogue to come to fruition.

So, the 'Hull Hebrew Congregation' became the sole guardian of Hull and District's Orthodox Judaism.

Hull Hebrew Synagogue, Pryme Street, Anlaby. Formally opened 2 April 1995.

A 'Pryme' Move

'To bring two (Jewish) organisations together is truly a miracle. Congregations often divide, they very seldom unite.'

Chief Rabbi, 2nd April, 1995 (Hull).

And with those prophetic words, the Chief Rabbi of the United Kingdom, Dr. Jonathan Sacks, began his speech at the formal opening of Hull's first new Orthodox Synagogue for more than 90 years, by name 'Hull Hebrew Congregation'.

The setting was Pryme Street, Anlaby, on the outskirts of Hull; the date, 2 April, 1995,[25] when the congregations of the 'Hull Western Synagogue' in Linnaeus Street, on Anlaby Road, amalgamated with the 'Hull Old Hebrew Synagogue', based in Osborne Street, in Hull's City centre.[26] The 'Old Hebrew' had been demolished; the 'Western,', was, tragically, an empty shell, so the day was indeed a turning point in the history of Hull's Orthodox Houses of Prayer.

In addition to the opening of the building came the induction of the Synagogue's first Rabbi, Shalom Osdoba, who aptly reminded his congregation that 'the source of Jewish life is not within the Synagogue but within us'. Twenty-eight-year-old Rabbi Osdoba had qualified at a Yeshiva[27] in New York's Lubavitch area.

The Chief Rabbi stressed the importance of the next generation, and congratulated both Rabbi Osdoba and Rebbetzin Sarah Osdoba on their sterling efforts with the young children's Jewish education. On a lighter note, Dr. Sacks amused the packed congregation when addressing the new young incumbent with the words, 'You are a young man, Rabbi Osdoba, a mere 28 years of age, but, as they said to me when I took on my first Rabbinic job, "You are a very young man for this community." I replied, "Don't worry. In *this* community I'll age rapidly!"' Some nervous laughter greeted the remark, but, like all truly good jokes (if joke it was), it hit a chord in a community whose previous inter-synagogue disagreements had been at times bitter and long-standing.

But this day was a *good* day. The future beckoned and the Synagogue President, Howard Levy, proudly announced that 'We (Hull) are the only Jewish community in Great Britain to formally open a new Synagogue this year (1995).' It heralded the dawn of a new religious era for Hull's 400-500 traditional Jews, who now, in the main, lived on the City's outskirts, compared with their parents and grandparents whose location was Hull's Old Town of some 50-100 years earlier.

The new Synagogue building, though much smaller than its predecessor, the 'Hull Western', managed effectively to combine the past with the present. The highly impressive Holy Ark had been brought from the 'Hull Western' – a momentous task which involved separation of the various sections, followed by a rebuilding operation in its new location. The newly-designed superlative windows, each with its own biblical theme, were created by Judy Sobin of London and the candelabra – again transported from the 'Hull Western' – added a further emotional memory of days gone by.

A unique privilege was bestowed on the Synagogue Executive, since they became, like their 18/19th-century predecessors at Posterngate, the leaders of the only existing Orthodox Synagogue to serve the Hull community. By name they were: Howard Levy (President), Philip Daniels (Vice-President), Anthony Rowland (Treasurer) and Edward Pearlman (Secretary), to which should be added the quartet of Wardens: Barrie Donn, Emmanuel (Manny) Marks – who, as mentioned earlier, died a year or so later – Judah Rose and Conrad Segelman. The Wardens' responsibility, in conjunction with the Rabbi, is to give vital assistance to the Synagogue Officers. Howard Levy paid a special tribute to his Vice-President, Philip Daniels, in respect of Philip's long-term dedication and hard work towards the realisation of the new venture.

After their sterling efforts with the administrative work behind the construction of the new Synagogue, Howard Levy and Philip Daniels understandably felt that their task was complete and a rest was called for, leaving vacancies as Synagogue President and Vice-President. Well-known Hull solicitor Max Gold stepped into the President's rôle, the Vice-President's position remaining vacant for some time. In October, 1997, Honorary Treasurer Anthony Rowland resigned, and the Max Gold-Edward Pearlman duo held the fort.

The current Executive quartet which has taken the Hull Hebrew synagogue into the new Millennium consists of: Max Gold (President), Barrie Donn, M.A. (Vice-President), Edward Pearlman (Honorary Treasurer) and Jonathan Levine (Honorary Secretary).

At the 1999 A.G.M., Synagogue Wardens Conrad Segelman and Judah Rose 'stood down' after completing their three-year tenancies of the position and Leslie Abrahams and Mott Levine replaced them, together with the existing Wardens, Stephan Pearlman and Alf Klarik, as the twenty-first century appeared on the horizon.

Rabbi Shalom Osdoba, Rebbetzin Sarah and children (1995).

Hull Hebrew Synagogue – Official Opening – April 1995.
L to r: E. Pearlman, A. Rowland, H. Levy, Chief Rabbi, P. Daniels.

Children of the Cheder.

And Finally . . .

'Less in numbers, but remarkably active'.

Max Gold, President Hull Hebrew Congregation (1999)

We began in 1780 with a minimal Jewish presence in Hull. This grew to around 2,000 or so in the first half of the 20th century. Although few educational opportunities were on offer at that time, the City of Hull was regarded by its Jewish community as a friendly place in which to spend one's life.

But, as the 'education for all' era arrived and, in consequence, opened up both university and additional social opportunities, Hull's Jewish teenagers and young married couples were attracted to the major Jewish centres of Manchester and London – hence unwittingly contributing to a steady decline in Hull's Jewish population, a common enough current provincial problem. The feelings of a typical Hull teenager, Beverley Rowland, summarises the situation for the young: 'Sometimes it can feel pretty lonely being 16 and Jewish and living in Hull, so to meet new friends from London and Manchester is great for sharing and having fun.'

In addition, the increasing age-profile of Hull's Jewry suggests that the future will bring a significantly smaller – but hopefully stable – Jewish presence in the City.

Synagogue President Max Gold effectively summed up the feelings of many with the words, 'We have a building admired by all who visit it, and look forward to many more years of promotion of Orthodox Judaism in Hull.'

Chief Rabbi, Dr. Jonathan Sacks, in his address at the opening of the new 'Hull Hebrew Synagogue', aptly remarked, 'The warmth of a Jewish community is in exact inverse proportion to its size. You don't *count* Jews, you make certain that every Jew *counts*.'

Hopefully, Dr. Sacks had Hull in mind!

One could, of course, go on indefinitely about the Hull Synagogues, past and present, together with the legion of congregants connected with them, but it's apt to end with a quote from the Talmud:

'He who multiplied his words will likely come to sin.'

Synagogue President Max Gold, and wife Laura, at a Mock Passover Function.

Jewish Education for the Young in Hull

'We do not think only about our past but about our future, and our future is our children'.
Chief Rabbi, 2 April, 1995 (Hull)

Historically, Jewish religious education has always been 'attached', both physically and morally, to its local place of worship.[28] Synagogues are expected to take responsibility – if only on a part-time basis – for providing the facilities for the advancement of Jewish knowledge to their young pupils.

It is worthy of note that when the approval of the Chief Rabbi was sought regarding the 'Hull Western Synagogue' project, in 1901, he refused such recognition unless a school was part of the complex. In his dual role of Synagogue President and Architect. Mr. B. S. Jacobs assured the Chief Rabbi that such a school would be built.

In Hull's case it is probable that Samuel Simon, originally Minister of the Parade Row Synagogue in 1809, became Hull's first religious education teacher. When the Robinson Row 'amalgamation' in 1826 took place, it included a school within the Synagogue's precincts; hence it accommodated the educational needs of the children from the former Posterngate and Parade Row Synagogues. Simon died in 1866 at the age of 85.

Extract from a Board of Deputies' report dated 13th February, 1853, when 15 boys and 14 girls were in attendance at Hull Hebrew Educational Society's school, Synagogue Buildings, Robinson Row:

Subjects taught

Boys	English, Commercial Education; Hebrew and Religious Education, instruction daily, arithmetic.
Girls	Hebrew and Religious Education twice weekly.
Paid Officer	Samuel Simon, Chasan and Shochet – Salary, £52 per annum. The Synagogue, in addition to owning the building itself, had some small tenements, one of which was occupied by Samuel Simon and was subject to a mortgage debt of £250, bearing interest of 5 per cent per annum.

Education was based on the 'Robin Hood' concept, i.e. support the weak (financially) against the strong, so that those parents who could afford the small fees involved would thereby enable the school governors to allow poorer families to send their children to school free of charge. Even school clothes were provided for the less well-off, which always proved to be the majority.

In addition, in the mid-19th century the name Philip Bender dominated in his dual role of Minister and teacher. A rare talent, he came from Germany and raised religious standards by his own effective preaching, allied to his inspirational teaching methods.

One of the Heads of the Jewish School, whose personal attainments went far beyond the confines of Hull, was Abraham Elzas. His translation of Biblical texts created considerable interest across the religious (Jewish/Christian) divide. He arrived from Holland in 1871, when he was 32 years of age, and died a relatively young man in 1880.

Other preachers of note, and presumably teachers of the Cheder, were: David Fay, Israel Levy, Ephraim Cohen, Henry David Marks, Elkan Epstein and Abraham Jacobs.

As mentioned earlier, the birth of the Western Synagogue, in 1902, went hand-in-hand with the creation of its adjacent school building, designed by the Synagogue's first President, Benjamin Septimus Jacobs. At a meeting of the Synagogue Council in 1903, satisfaction was expressed at the school's progress, 'the most successful out of London'.

Mrs. Isabel Jacobs, wife of B. S. Jacobs, was President of the Hull Hebrew Girls' School for nearly 20 years. Like her highly-respected husband, she was involved in a vast array of voluntary work, including membership of both the Jewish Ladies' Benevolent Society for 25 years and the Hull Jubilee District Nursing Association.

Miss Annie Shinerog became Head Teacher of the Jewish Girls' School in its early years. As a leading player in the long cast of Cheder teachers, Miss Shinerog proved a strict disciplinarian, (as many of her past pupils will confirm), but a strong-willed lady dedicated to her important task during a period when the number of girls could well have topped the 200 mark, in a 'full-time' school, compared with the current handful of Cheder pupils who study on a 'part-time' basis. (Miss Shinerog's predecessor had been Miss Magner, who, with equal determination and loyalty, was Head Teacher during the Synagogue's early days of the 20th century.)

In general, Jewish boys attended State schools, withdrawing from the daily act of Christian worship, and acquiring their Jewish religious education – and preparation for their Barmitzvah – at the Western Synagogue Cheder (and at a later stage at other venues) on Sundays and weekday evenings, with memorable teachers such as 'Pecky' Gordon, Reverend 'Hymie' Davies, and Messrs. Ostroff, Citron and Segal, who are still spoken of with gratitude and affection to this very day, some half century later. The list is seemingly endless: Rabbi Rabinowitz,[29] Rabbi Dr. Cooper, Rabbi Broder, Reverend Freedberg, Reverend Caplan, Reverend Willencyk, Reverend Hirsch.

Leslie Abrahams, Michael Westerman, Audrey Segelman, Len Utal, Jack Powell and Lionel Charnah all featured in the list of Head Teachers and staff of the various Cheders.

In an article in 1931, entitled *The Hull Hebrew School, its Aims and Work,* Headmaster Reverend David Hirsch wrote, 'Holy Writ enjoins upon us the sacred duty of instructing the young, and primarily places this obligation on the parents. As an adjunct of such home instruction, *but by no means as a substitute for it,* the teacher and his school was given the place of first importance by the Rabbis from earliest times. Jews have taken to heart the Rabbinic adage, "There is no one so poor as a man who is wanting in knowledge."'

A sincere appeal 'to aid us by sending your boys and girls – and by your liberal financial assistance – so that all children, rich and poor alike, may receive the blessing of Jewish education', signified a period in the 1930s when Hull Jewish education leaders were striving to attract in excess of 150 pupils to attend the cheder, as opposed to the 1990s, when such numbers have long gone.

.A letter from Headmaster Reverend David Hirsch dated 2 July, 1933, to the Treasurer, Mr. Louis Rapstone, was fairly typical of the kindly manner in which such schools were organised when financial considerations were under review. The letter read: 'This lad has *not* been paying fees for a considerable time, and the reason given each time is that his father is out of work. According to the lad, the father has been out of work for three years and is keeping his family out of his dole money. I shall be glad to know whether, as Treasurer, you are satisfied with the lad to continue on the free list?'

The reply from Mr. Rapstone accepted that, after inquiries, Reverend Hirsch's facts appeared correct, but that it was 'a case where we should teach the boy free, and I am quite satisfied personally'.

Hull-born John Wilson, who has lived in the City all his life, and is now in his 90th year, fondly remembers his boyhood years at Cheder. With John's help – and a soupçon of imagination – a typical Cheder classroom (strictly boys only) of the 1920s to 1930s may well have looked like this:

Annis	Bentley	Chapel	Cuckle	Back
Fredenthal	Gerson	Goodman	Harris	
Korklin	Lieberman	Lipman	Marks	
Palmer	Rapstone	Rosenthal	Shenker	
Silverstone	Sugar	Sugarman	Turner	
Waxman	Westerman	Wilson	Wineberg	Front

Teacher: Mr. 'Pecky' Gordon

The outbreak of the 1939-45 War saw the demise of the Hull Jewish Girls' School in Linnaeus Street. Nowadays, even to contemplate a revival of a Jewish School in Hull would prove a non-starter, due to the progressively smaller numbers of children available from Hull's Jewish population, which has been in severe decline for some years past.

Rabbi and Rebbetzin Osdoba, with Laurette Pearlman, are currently (1999) in charge of the Jewish education of an 'all-age' Cheder (five to twelve years) at the Hull Hebrew Congregation Community Centre in Pryme Street, Anlaby, with no more than ten or so pupils and the consequent educational difficulties which such a variation of ages is bound to bring. This, of course, must prove somewhat of a struggle, compared with education in 'all-Jewish' schools in the larger Jewish communities of Leeds, Manchester and London.

In the early years, in spite of the typical Jewish family being among the lowest wage-earners in the country (jobs in the 'non-professional' classes being their only means of earning a living wage), parents considered the education of their children, even well beyond the school compulsory leaving age, of paramount importance.

Sixth-form and university education, which had been denied immigrant parents, became a 'must' for their children, even though the consequence was less money coming into the household as children extended their education at the expense of paid work – I write from grateful personal experience!

Hull Hebrew Communal School, Summer 1958 – Visit of Chief Rabbi.
Middle Row: Len Utal, Louis Harris, Rabbi Rabinowitz, Jack Powell, Issy Appleson, Dr. Lurie, Lady Brodie, Sir Israel Brodie, Louis Rapstone, Rev. Willencyk, Rev. Davies, Rev. Freedberg.

SPEECH OF CHIEF RABBI DR. JONATHAN SACKS AT THE OPENING OF THE NEW HULL HEBREW CONGREGATION SYNAGOGUE, PRYME STREET, ANLABY on 2 April, 1995

Worshipful Mayor of Beverley and Mayoress of Beverley, Lord Mayor of Hull and Lady Mayoress of Hull, local MPs, distinguished Dyanim and Rabbonim, Bishop of Hull and other distinguished visitors, Ladies and Gentlemen.

This is a delightful day, praise G-d, and we rejoice in Him. What a very special occasion it is, standing as we are between Shabbat and Rosh Chodesh! Shabbat we celebrated yesterday, the Shabbat in the new month; not only in the new month of Nisan but a new era in the life of this 'Hull Hebrew Congregation'; and the coming Shabbat is the 'Great Shabbat' in which the Jewish people re-dedicated themselves prior to the Exodus from Egypt. You are re-dedicating yourselves through this new Shul and under the new leadership of your delightful new Rabbi, Rabbi Osdoba.

Chief Rabbi.

It is a long drive from London – although as I kept seeing the signs that said, 'Services 35 miles', I knew I was on the right road for a Shul! As we were making the long trip north, I reminded myself that the Hebrew word for 'north', which is 'tsafon', also means a hidden treasure. You know, the Afikomen that we hide on Pesach (Passover) is also called 'tsafon', which means a treasure which is hidden, and that, I think, is precisely true of this Jewish community – the treasure that deserves to be much more widely known, and for three obvious reasons:

First of all, of course, is the miracle represented by this new Shul building. The Midrash tells us that a Roman lady 1900 years ago asked a very good question of the great rabbi, Rabbi Akiva. She said, 'Rabbi, you believe that the Almighty created the world and the whole universe in seven days. Tell me, what has He been doing since?' Rabbi Akiva gave a very remarkable answer: 'He sits and arranges marriages.' (Please G d by all our children!). And the Roman lady said, 'You think that is difficult? That is easy!' But Rabbi Akiva said, 'To bring two Jews together is as difficult as dividing the Red Sea!', and if you can imagine *that* it is difficult, to bring two *individuals* together, then to bring two *congregations* together, this is truly a miracle! Congregations often divide; they very seldom unite, yet here in this new Hull Hebrew Congregation you have done just that – brought together two old and very distinguished congregations and built this splendid new Shul, and with it truly you have brought a new lease of life to this great Jewish community.

Then there is, of course, something else about Hull: it is a community that values the Jewish tradition, the Jewish heritage, and not only values it, but *lives* it as well. Given the size of your population, your average Shabbat percentage attendance must be one of the very highest in the country.

You have so clearly understood the fundamental axiom of our heritage, which is that what we *take* from Judaism depends on what we *give* to it, and you are willing to give to Jewish life as well as asking it to *give* to you.

Thirdly, of course, and perhaps the most important, you have understood the vital truth – and please never forget – that a *small* community can still be a *great* community. I must tell you that it is a remarkable phenomenon which I have observed so many times (so many times that I have now been able to formulate it in a theorem which I call 'Sack's Law') which says the following: The warmth of the community is in exact inverse proportion to its size. You can have a large, large community which can be anonymous, it can be cold; then you have a small community like this one, where every single individual feels valued. You know, it is an unusual Jewish principle, and you find it really spelled out in the saying that, "You do not *count* Jews . . . however you count them, you do not directly count them." The question is, why? Why don't we count Jews? The answer is simple – whenever a group takes a census, it is tempted to believe that its strength depends on its size, that its strength lies in numbers. We, as a Jewish people, know otherwise; our strength has never, ever, lain in numbers. For the last 200 years we have been less than one-half per cent of the population of the world. We have always been a tiny people, even from the days of Moshe Rebbenu, who said . . . "You are the smallest of all people." We are a *tiny people*, and yet our influence has always been vast, because our strength never depended on numbers.

What, then, is it we do instead of *counting* Jews? Instead of that, we make sure that *every* Jew *counts*, and that you have done.

Here in Hull you have much to be proud of, much to give you confidence in the future. This magnificent new building; your new sense of community, and, above all, your new Rabbi, whom I induct today. This will give you a new lease of life, and may you truly celebrate the 'Shabbat of Renewal', not only today but every Shabbat for many years to come.

In choosing Rabbi Osdoba as your new Rabbi, you have chosen well, and already in the short time you have been here, Rabbi Osdoba, you have acquired a 'shem tov', a 'good name' and a fine reputation. You, along with your delightful wife and two lovely daughters (and how thrilled we are to see your father here today and parents-in-law and many other members of the family) have already endeared yourself to the community. Indeed, even those people who were just a little eyebrow-raising – shall we put it – at one or two of your suggestions earlier on have now become your friends, and therefore you have practised that most wonderful virtue: *'Who is truly mighty? . . . He who turns a critic into a friend.'*

Together, Rabbi Osdoba, you and your wife have revitalised much in this community. You have created between the two of you a lovely programme of Shiurim (meeting with a religious theme); you have established a Sunday morning Minyan, which I am only sorry I missed this morning, because I gather it has smoked salmon, cream cheese and no less then *four* varieties of bagels! You have initiated a most delightful Shul newsletter, *The Pryme News*, which it is a pleasure to read; but, of course, most important of all – and I hope the community here understands how important it is and how astonishingly well you have done – you have revitalised the Cheder. I was so moved when, before coming into the Shul just now, I was able to sit for half-an-hour with the children of the Cheder and hear them so beautifully sing about Shabbat; to act out their roles and to see their faces shining, shining with love for the things that they have been taught. And I must tell you that every one of you in this community should 'shlep nachas' – I don't know what that is in English – in English you don't 'shlep nachas' – but you should really take pride and pleasure in these lovely children of yours, and I imagine that your Rabbi and Rebbetzin have already achieved this.

Rabbi Osdoba, you are a young man, although, as they said to me when I took on my first rabbinic job at your age, 'Rabbi, you are very young for this community'; and I said, 'Don't worry. In this community *I will age rapidly*!' You are a young man, Rabbi Osdoba, a mere 28 years old, and, as you know, the Hebrew for 28 spells out the word '*koach*', which means '*strength*'. May you always have strength in yourself; may you radiate strength to others, and may you give this community strength for many years to come.

Let me conclude with a very simple thought which is to you, Rabbi Osdoba, my challenge and my blessing: We say a very striking thing in a couple of weeks' time when we come to sit round the Seder[30] table and we say that every one of us has to feel as if we personally left Egypt and we personally pray. I just want us to reflect for a moment on why this is:

It is a remarkable thing which, oddly enough, I have never seen anyone comment on, but it is a stunning fact. We, the Jewish people, are a people of history; we have a history longer than most – three-quarters of the history of human civilization – and more remarkable than almost any other. What is more, we were the first people in human civilization ever to see G-d in history; to see meaning and pattern and shape in history. And, indeed, on Pesach we recall events that happened some 3,200, or more, years ago. Given, therefore, the astonishing history that we have, is it not remarkable that there is no word in the Hebrew language for 'history'?

It is so glaring an omission that when modern Hebrew scholars searched for a word for 'history' they had to borrow it from the English, which borrowed it from the Latin, which borrowed it from the Greek, so the modern Hebrew word for 'history' is 'historia'!

What do we have instead of 'history'? I will tell you. There is one word that occurs again and again, no less than 169 times in the Hebrew Bible: the word '*zachor*', and the word '*zachor*' means not '*history*' but '*memory*' . . . What we do on Pesach is not history, it is memory. What is the difference? The difference is very simple: 'history' is *his story*; 'history' is something that happened to *somebody else at some time else*. 'History' did not happen to me. '*Memory*', however, is *my story*; if I can remember something, then it is at least *as if* it happened to me. And that is why on Pesach we do not tell the story of the coming out of Egypt as a history lesson; instead, we re-live it, we re-enact it. We *eat* the bread of affliction, we *taste* the bitter herbs of slavery, we *drink* the four cups of freedom. We do not *talk* about the past, we *live it* until it becomes not something that happened long ago and far away, but it becomes something that has meaning for me, for here and for now.

. . . We have to see it as if we personally experienced the Exodus, because we believe not in history but in memory. This is the great challenge of a Rav (Rabbi). It is to take our magnificent, awe-inspiring history and make it live in the here and now; in the hearts of every single member of this congregation; to turn history into memory, to turn the past into a living present.

Because of this, it is no coincidence whatsoever that on Pesach, specially, when we are so conscious of all we are as a people, we cannot tell that story, the story of the Haggadah,[31] until questions have been asked by a *child*. And as we do not only have history but we also have memory, we do not think only about our past but about our future, and our future is our children. Because of that, the most ancient people, almost, in human history, remain the youngest people as well: and that is why the most important task of a Rav is to endow the next generation with *zachor*, with Jewish memories, so that new generations of this community feel that Judaism means something personally to them.

That is my blessing to you, Rabbi Osdoba, that you, in this wonderful renewed 'Hull Hebrew Congregation', make Judaism come alive for this community, and especially its children. May you turn the great history of Jewish life in Hull into a set of new and unforgettable memories, and may you add to the already distinguished past of this congregation a yet more distinguished future. Amen

HULL HEBREW CONGREGATION

ORDER OF SERVICE
at the
CONSECRATION
of the
HULL HEBREW SYNAGOGUE and
COMMUNITY CENTRE
and the
INDUCTION
of
RABBI SHALOM OSDOBA
by
The Chief Rabbi
Dr. JONATHAN SACKS
on
Sunday 2nd April 1995
2 Nisan 5755
at 4.00 pm.
The Service will be conducted by Mr. David Rose

Copy of Service . . . .

ORDER OF SERVICE

The first page number refers to the centenary edition of the Singer's Prayer Book, the second page number (in brackets) refers to the previous edition of the Singer's Prayer Book.

"How goodly are thy tents, O Jacob"........................ מה־טבו Page 1(1)

The Ark is opened.

Entry of Sifrei Torah (Scrolls of the Law) to:-

"Blessed is he that comes"................................ ברוך הבא Page 593 (300)

"Whenever the ark".. ויהי בנסע Page 361(193)

The Scrolls are placed in the Ark

"And when the Ark".. ובנחה יאמר Page 391 (210)

The Ark is closed.

::

The congregation sits.

Psalm 30 Read by the Chazan.......... מזמור שיר חנכת הבית Page 33 (16)

Psalm 121 Sung by the Chazan and congregation....................................
שיר למעלות Page 463 (245)

Psalm 122 Read in unison in English by the congregation..........................
שיר המעלות Page 465 (245)

::

Afternoon Service.. מנחה Page 157 (99)

::

"I will praise You".. אודך Page 591 (299)

Reading by Dayan Osdoba of Psalm 93...................... ה׳ מלך Page 235 (148)

Reading by Rabbi Dr. Cooper Emeritus Rabbi - Zohar............................
בריך שמה Page 363 (194)

Prayer for the consecration of the Synagogue.

Prayer for the Congregation "May He who blessed".......... מי שברך Page 379(203)

Prayer for the Queen and the Royal Family..
תפלה לשלום המלכות Page 381(203)

Prayer for the welfare of the State of Israel...
תפלה לשלום מדינת ישראל Page 381 (204)

::

Address by the Chief Rabbi

Address by Rabbi Shalom Osdoba

::

"It is our duty"...עלינו לשבח Page 415 (221)

Kaddish...יתגדל Page 417(222)

::

Welcome from the President of the Congregation Howard Levy

::

The Service concludes with the singing of "Lord of the universe"............................
אדון עולם Page 9 (4)

Congregants are kindly requested to remain in their places until the Chief Rabbi, Officiants, Honorary Officers and Distinguished Guests have left the Synagogue.

LIST OF JEWISH MAYORS, LORD MAYORS AND SHERIFFS OF HULL

1890	John Symons	Sheriff
1902	Victor Dumoulin	Sheriff
1905	Edward Gosschalk	Sheriff
1906-7-8-9	Henry Feldman	Mayor
1910	Edward Dumoulin	Sheriff
1923, 1932, 1939	Benno Pearlman	Sheriff
1928	Benno Pearlman	Lord Mayor
1942	Joseph Leopold Schultz*	Lord Mayor
1951	Lionel Rosen	Sheriff
1952	Alfed Kyno Jacobs	Lord Mayor
1958	Lawrence Science	Lord Mayor
1959	Lawrence Science	Lord Mayor
1972	Lionel Rosen	Lord Mayor
1983	Louis Pearlman	Lord Mayor

Hull had Mayors until 1914.

* Knighted in 1966.

Alderman H. Feldman, J.P., Mayor of Hull 1906-07-08-09.

LIST OF SYNAGOGUE OFFICERS
HULL WESTERN SYNAGOGUE
Founded 1901

PRESIDENTS

1901-26	B. S. JACOBS
1926-29	BENN FRANKS
1929-41	H. ROSENSTON
1941-44	J. LEWENSTEIN
1944-70	DR. S. LURIE
1970-75	N. ROSENSTON
1975-80	C. SEGELMAN, M.Sc.
1980-83	E. MARKS
1983-85	J. ROSE
1985-87	H. COHEN
1987-91	C. J. ROSENSTON B.A., F.C.A.
1991-94	P. H. DANIELS, B.Sc.
	H. J. LEVY

VICE-PRESIDENTS

1901-15	H. FELDMAN
1915-19	L. H. BERGMAN
1919-21	BENN FRANKS
1921-23	D. LIPINSKI
1923-25	BENN FRANKS
1925-29	M. V. GOSSCHALK
1929-30	J. AARON
1930-42	H. R. SCIENCE
1942-43	D. L. JACOBS
1943-44	DR. S. LURIE
1944-55	J. LEWENSTEIN
1955-70	L. HARRIS, M.B.E.
1970-75	C. SEGELMAN, B.Sc.
1975-76	R. G. FIELD, F.C.A.
1976	W. SUGARMAN, M.C.
1977-80	E. MARKS
1980-83	M. BLACK
1983-85	H. COHEN
1985-91	DR. C. ROSEN
(WARDEN)	

HON. TREASURER

1901-09	J. MAGNER
1909-20	B. I. BARNARD
1920-26	N. GOLDSTONE
1926-29	JOS. BUSH
1929-30	I. BERGMAN
1930-34	JOS. BUSH
1934-36	S. ZIMMERMAN
1936-42	S. GOLDREIN
1942-55	S. ZIMMERMAN
1955-58	L. A. ABRAHAMS
1958-62	H. COHEN
1962-68	N. ROSENSTON
1968-70	C. SEGELMAN M.Sc.
1970-75	R. G. FIELD, F.C.A.
1975-76	M. FIELD
1976-80	J. LEWIN
1980-82	H. LANCH, B.A.
1982-83	J. E. FINESTEIN, LL.B.
1983-84	P. H. DANIELS, B.Sc.
1984-85	B. FIDLER, LL.B.
1985-87	C. J. ROSENSTON B.A., F.C.A.
1987-91	E. BENNETT
1991-94	A. ROWLAND, F.C.A.

HON. SECRETARY

1901-15	L. H. BERGMAN
1915-21	M. V. GOSSCHALK
1921-26	J. BUSH
1926-28	T. G. VICE, A.C.A.
1928-29	D. L. JACOBS
1929-37	E. LEVINSON
1937-43	L. BARNETT
1943-49	M. FIELD
1949-53	I. S. SCHULTZ
1953-55	H. MARCH
1955-58	W. SUGARMAN, M.C.
1958-68	C. SEGELMAN, B.Sc.
1968-69	H. LANCH, B.A.
1969-70	M. KOSKIE
1970-75	W. SUGARMAN, M.C.
1975-77	J. ROSE
1977-80	H. LANCH, B.A.
1980-83	P. H. DANIELS, B.Sc.
1983-87	L. F. KAUFFMAN
1987-91	H. J. LEVY
1991-94	E. PEARLMAN

LIST OF SYNAGOGUE OFFICERS
HULL OLD HEBREW CONGREGATION
Established 1826

PRESIDENTS

1903-07	MARCUS CASRIL
1907-26	J. E. COHEN (LIFE PRESIDENT 1926-27)
1924-26	ISRAEL BENTLEY (CHAIRMAN)
1926-28	MYER MILLER
1928-31	JACK LEVY
1931-40	D. M. ROSEN
1940-58	L. RAPSTONE
1958-63	H. M. BENTLEY
1964	H. ROSEN
1965-75	H. M. BENTLEY
1975-80	G. GOLD
1980-85	H. TAYLOR
1986	H. SCHULMAN
1987-94	B. DONN, M.A.

VICE-PRESIDENTS

1945-58	A. LAVINE
1958-63	H. ROSEN
1965-67	H. ROSEN
1968-74	G. GOLD
1975-85	H. SCHULMAN
1986-94	C. MARKS

HON. TREASURERS

1903-07	J. E. COHEN
1907-20	J. E. ROSENTHAL
1920-26	JACK LEVY
1926-46	L. RAPSTONE
1946-50	D. ROBINSON
1950-58	J. ROSEN
1959-61	J. W. FINESTEIN
1962-80	H. TAYLOR
1980-85	C. MARKS
1986-93	I. MICHAELS
1993-94	H. SCHULMAN

HON.SECRETARIES

1903	B. PEARLMAN
1903-05	D. MOSS
1905-09	B. H. JESSEL
1909-10	ALFRED CASRIL
1910-15	D. M. ROSEN
1915-20	PHINEAS HART
1918-20	R. MARKS (JOINT HON. SEC.)
1920-45	BARNETT GOLDSTONE
1945-48	VICTOR MARKS
1948-56	L. FINESTEIN
1956-63	D. SILVERSTONE B.A.
1964-75	H. SCHULMAN
1975-87	B. DONN, M.A.
1987-94	M. J. GOLD

Officers of the Congregation – Consecration of the Synagogue, 1 September 1955.

President:
L. Rapstone

Vice-President:
A. Levine

Hon. Treasurer:
J. Rosen

Hon. Secretary:
L. Finestein

The Synagogue as a Communal Centre

Naturally, a Synagogue is, above all, a House for Prayer, but in a small Jewish community, of which present-day Hull is one, its lone Orthodox Synagogue must always serve as a Communal Centre for social activities in addition to its three regular daily services, namely: Shachris (morning), Mincha (afternoon, before sunset), and Maariv (evening).

On Sabbaths and Festivals, an additional service, known as Mussaph, is added, usually recited after the morning Shachris service.

(a) THE HULL JEWISH REPRESENTATIVE COUNCIL

'How good and how pleasant it is when brethren dwell together in harmony.'

Founded in February 1945, towards the end of World War II, The Hull Jewish Representative Council presents an over-view of the local Jewish Community in all its relations with the Hull public, Jew and non-Jew alike.

Among its affiliated organisations, both past and present, are listed: Hull Western Synagogue, Old Hebrew Congregation, Central Synagogue, Hull Reform Synagogue, Hull Hebrew Schools, the current Hebrew Synagogue and a veritable host of committee and societies.

While basically existing as an 'umbrella' organisation, the Hull Jewish Representative Council has nevertheless taken individual responsibility for exhibitions in Hull's City centre as varied as: The Jewish Way of Life (1985), The Life of Anne Frank, The 50th Anniversary of the State of Israel (1998) and a Jewish slant on Kingston upon Hull's 700th Anniversary (1999) of the granting of its Charter by King Edward I. The venue was Hull's Maritime Museum, in October 1999, less than three months before the arrival of a new Millennium.

The official organ of the Representative Council is a fortnightly newspaper entitled *Hull Jewish Watchman,* which has recently celebrated its 1,000th issue.

An article in 'Issue 1000', written by Judah Rose, a past editor of the 'Watchman', with connections over many years, lists previous editors for deserved praise.

The late Rabbi E. S. Rabinowitz provided the initial inspiration, with Bernard Levy as the publication's first editor. The list continues: Rabbi C. J. Cooper, David Passman, Lloyd Levy and, currently, an editorial committee sharing the load, and providing a whole variety of local and national features of Jewish interest to readers in Hull, and further afield.

The abiding message that each edition carries to its readers is at the head of this resumé.

(b) THE 'PRYME NEWS'

Introduced by Rabbi Shalom Osdoba in 1995, the 'Pryme News' is a monthly pamphlet which covers all religious aspects of the 'Hull Hebrew Congregation'.

It combines both serious and amusing articles, added to invitations to celebrate a variety of Jewish festivals held at the Rabbi's home, adjoining the Synagogue, with Rebbetzin Sarah Osdoba and her many willing helpers providing an informal and unpretentious atmosphere, and serving post-morning-service meals, a welcome successor to similar style functions which Lionel and Rita Charnah organised for many years in the past.

The ultimate accolade to the 'Pryme News' came from Chief Rabbi Jonathan Sacks, at Rabbi Osdoba's induction as 'Hull Hebrew Synagogues' religious leader, in April 1995.

'It is indeed a pleasure to read,' said Dr. Sacks.

(c) HULL AND DISTRICT COUNCIL OF CHRISTIANS AND JEWS (HULL C.C.J.)

A variety of functions under the auspices of the Council of Christians and Jews (Hull Branch) have been held in the various Synagogues over more than 50 years.

The National C.C.J. came into being in London during the 1939-45 War when man-of-his-time Winston Churchill, revered by Jew and non-Jew alike, inspired a nation to repel the possible Nazi invasion of this country. British Jews, especially, saw the appalling cruelty suffered by the Jewish Holocaust victims as the possible shape of things to come if Britain was ever to succumb to Hitler's threats.

In 1942, Chief Rabbi J. H. Hertz and the Archbishop of Canterbury, William Temple, together with leaders of many other religious denominations, joined together in a common effort to promote mutual understanding between the faiths. Past differences, held over many years, even centuries, were replaced by a more positive outlook whereby *Common Ground* (the title of C.C.J.'s magazine) took precedence, and additional knowledge of each other's religions became a priority.

The local movement began in 1947 and gained momentum under the leadership of past Jewish Lord Mayor of Hull Lionel Rosen and C.C.J.'s London representative, Canon Foster. Civic patronage began with the then Lord Mayor of Hull, Alderman T. R. Broadbent, and has continued ever since, with the A.G.M.s being held in the splendour of the Hull Guildhall Reception Room.

Well-known local people from both sides of the River Humber have served as Executive members, including, from Hull: Judah Rose and the late Jack Lennard, and from Winterton on the South Bank of the Humber, Ann Eccleston.

Chairmen, in recent years, include the present incumbent, Barbara Robinson, her predecessors being Andrew Carrick and Michael Westerman. I have served as the Treasurer for the past twelve years, and Joan Fredenthal is Secretary. Dr. Lionel North, from the Theology Department of Hull University, Dr. Michael Sanders, Rabbi Shalom Osdoba, the Reverend Alan Scrivener and the late Rabbi Dr. C. J. Cooper have served as executive members.

The Synagogues have played host to functions as varied as: Mock Seders (Passover), 'Any Questions?' and 'How and What to Cook for Jewish Festivals' by Rebbetzin Sarah Osdoba.

Notable speakers have included the Director of the National C.C.J., Sister Margaret Shepherd, the former Bishop of Hull, the Rt. Rev. James Jones (now Bishop of Liverpool),

Passover function.

and Dr. Elizabeth Maxwell on 'Why I believe that local branches of the C.C.J. and the National Council are among the most powerful secret weapons against anti-Semitism'.

It may be that our local branch does little more than scratch the surface of religious intolerance – unfortunately a current world-wide phenomenon.

To quote Mme. De Staël, '*Tout comprendre rend très indulgent*' – 'To know all makes one tolerant.'

We will never know *all* at Hull C.C.J., but for the sake of further generations of Christians and Jews in Hull (and further afield), we will continue to travel the road to further mutual knowledge and understanding.

Our aims, both nationally and locally, are summarised in the words: 'The Council brings together the Christian and Jewish communities in a common effort to fight the evils of prejudice, intolerance and discrimination between people of different religions, races and colours, and to work for the betterment of human relations based on mutual respect, understanding and goodwill. It is neither a missionary nor a political organisation.'

(d) HULL A.J.E.X)

A vitally important event in the Synagogue calendar occurs each November, when the City of Hull, represented by the Lord Mayor and other civic dignitaries, assemble in the morning at the Hull Cenotaph to conduct a Remembrance Day service in memory of the fallen of two World Wars. The Hull Association of Jewish Ex-Service Men and Women (Hull A.J.E.X.) conduct their service in the afternoon of the same day at the Synagogue, usually in the presence of civic leaders.

Pte. S. Abrahamson
Pte. J. Arronovitch
Pte. M. Black
Pte. B. Borodesky
Pte. A. Brown
Sgt. C. Bass
F/Sgt. C. Bentley
F/Sgt. G. Cobden
Pte. L. Cuckle
Pte. N. Ellis
Pte. S. Ellis
Pte. M. Feldman
Lieut. L. Franks
Cyc. H. Furman
Pte. H. Garfunkle
Cpl. D. Gordon
Lieut. E. Gosschalk
Sgt. W. Hare
F/Sgt. H. Harris
Capt. L. G. R. Harris
Pte. M. Hartstone
Pte, E. Hoffman
Capt, L. Holt
Gnr. H. Jessell
CQMS. D. Juggler
F/Man. A. Schooler
Pte. M. Kaye
Sig. B. Korklin
Pte. S. Levine
Pte. L. Levy
L/Cpl, A. Miller
Pte. M. Morack
AC/1 M. Moses
Pte. A. Moss
Capt. L. Newman
Pte. L. Newman
Pte. J. Opet
2/Lieut. D. Quesky
Bdr. F. Rapstone
Pte. I. Reubin
F/O H. Rathbone
Gnr. C. Rosenthall
A/C R. Rosenthall
Sgt. R. Schneer
Lieut. G. Scott-Forbes
Pte. B. Shalgosky
Pte. L. Slimmer
Eng. J. Stone
Pte. S. Sugarman
Pte. J. Sultan
P/Off. B. Tallerman

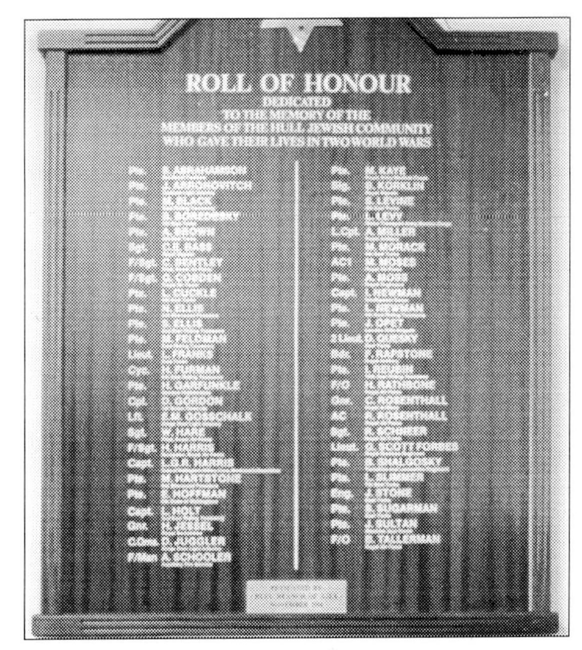

Founded in 1921, the Hull A.J.E.X., in the words of its present Chairman, Perris Coupland, has as its main aims, 'Remembrance, welfare, Jewish defence, social service and community relations'.

For many years, until the journey proved too weary, a Hull A.J.E.X. contingent went on parade past the London Cenotaph, with their Jewish brethren from all parts of the U.K. A religious service by the Chief Rabbi, and a march-past, taken by eminent high-ranking officers, followed.

It is apt to list the names of the fallen as seen on the Roll of Honour (see previous page) which is displayed on the rear wall of the Hull Hebrew Synagogue. Kindly donated by A.J.E.X. member, the late Moishe Furman, it reads, 'Dedicated to the Memory of the Members of the Hull Jewish Community who gave their lives in two World Wars'

(e) **THE LADIES**

'Your women-folk are the keepers of your homes, they are your sanctuaries; cause not a woman to weep, for G-d counts her tears; she is cherished, honoured and esteemed, and the glory of Jewish womanhood enhanced.' The Talmud

The above is a quote from Miss B. Berks in an article she wrote, in 1931, for a Hull magazine entitled *Palestine and Hebrew Board of Guardians.* Writing on behalf of the 'Palestine Women and Children's Welfare Society', it epitomised, to perfection, the role played by successive generations of Jewish 'committee ladies', often unsung, always essential!

(A)

(B)

Mesdames: L. Bennett, M. Bennett, C. Chappell, H. Edelson, S. Lavine, B. Feldman, J. W. Finestein, G. Gold, C. Hart, S. Lang, I. Lipman, J. Rosen, Cynthia Rosen, Lorna Rosen, A. Rosenblum, S. R. Sheffrin, H. Taylor, G. Vinegrad, Gertrude Vinedrad, H. Wilson.

To state some names, at the expense of others, would need an act of courage well beyond that of this book's author. Suffice it to say that the weekly Kiddush, after the Shabbat morning service, is dependent on the ladies' continued efforts; and the variety of societies which they organise, mostly of a charitable nature, are synagogue-based and, as Miss Berks wrote, enhance Jewish womanhood. Miss B. Berks is in the centre of the bottom row in picture (A) on previous page. The lower picture (B) was taken 25 years later at the re-opening of the 'Old Hebrew Synagogue' in 1955.

(f) SPORT

Many Hull Synagogue members, past and present, have ensured the presence of Hull Jewish representation in a variety of sports, of which table tennis and cricket probably lead the field.

Table Tennis

The 1930s saw the birth of Hull Judeans' Table Tennis Association, under the chairmanship of Eric Palmer, assisted by the late Gus Sugarman and Max Taylor.

The Hull Hebrew School, situated in the grounds of the Hull Western Synagogue, provided adequate table tennis facilities for the 'A Team', who went on to win many honours. In 1937/38, the side included: Abe Abrahamson, Cyril Brown, Jack Levy, Geoff Levy and Dennis Queskey.

Dennis – who became men's doubles champion of Hull with Cyril Brown – was capped for Yorkshire at the tender age of 15, the first Hull player to be so honoured. His sporting talents also included his prowess at Rugby Union, but the Dennis Queskey story was tragically cut short when, in September, 1944, soon after the D-Day landings in Normandy, he was killed in action at a mere 21 years of age. As a member of the 7th Battalion of the East Yorkshire Regiment, Dennis had speedily risen to the rank of lieutenant. The Hull community at large and his table tennis colleagues in particular, were left to grieve his loss. Dennis is buried in the Leopoldsburg war cemetery in Belgium.

Dennis's sister, Norma Queskey, continued the family table tennis tradition as a leading member of the Hull Area Yorkshire Team, winning a host of honours from 1946 to 1950. The seemingly endless list includes: Hull Closed Women's Singles, Women's Doubles and Mixed Doubles with her husband, Marcus Bishop, as partner. Norma died in Manchester in 1994.

The Hull Men's 'B Team' comprised: Marcus Bishop, Ivan Winetroube, Bernard Flasher, Maurice Segal, Max Taylor and Harold Harris, who was also killed in action. Occasional players were Joe Baczeles (an Austrian refugee), Eddie Brown, Lawrence Finestein, Jeremiah Krushevski and Morris Miller.

Post-war, Perris Coupland and the late Leon Rosenthal were leading players.

Bottom row centre: Abe Abrahamson.

Hull Judeans' doyen of table tennis is Abe Abrahamson. Abe represented Yorkshire on no fewer than seven occasions, before and after the 1939-45 War, with his appearance in the World Championship at the Royal Albert Hall, in London, in January, 1938, topping an illustrious career. Abe was deservedly made Life President of the Hull and District Table Tennis Association.

Cricket

'Mighty things from small beginnings grow' is a quote from the works of John Dryden and, allowing for some poetic licence, could well apply to the beginnings of sport, Hull Judeans' style, in Hull.

The 1914-1918 War was over when, in 1919, a few months after the conflict had ceased, a more restrained and far more pleasant activity began in Hull, namely cricket!

A journalist on the *Hull Evening News*, Simon Clyne, became Hull Judeans Cricket Club's first Chairman; Vice-Chairman was 'Wass' Silverstone, Treasurer, Henry Friedenthal, and Secretary, Gerry Greenstone.

As Hull Cricket Club's top team of the era played ON Anlaby Road Circle, so Hull Judeans pitched their wickets BEHIND the Circle, a somewhat less distinguished playing area, but the players' sense of commitment to the game was no less total!

At the Hull Judeans Cricket Club's 'Barmitzvah' Dinner in 1932, names memorable to readers whose twenty-first birthdays are at least 40 years ago, were: Motte Rubin (Umpire); Lionel Rosen (who became both Sheriff and Lord Mayor of Hull); schoolmaster Aubrey Gordon, Jack Marks, Harold Cuckle, Cecil Chapel, Josh Levy, Issy Appleson, Johnny Coupland, Sam and Leon Rosenthal, Manny Marks, and a host of others spanning several decades.

Sport in general broke down the barriers among the Hull Synagogues, as players from all three represented Hull Judeans C.C.

Eric Palmer, already mentioned in the Table Tennis section, held official appointments both as Assistant Secretary and then Secretary, replacing Gerry Greenstone.

Due to falling numbers, unfortunately, Hull Judeans C.C. went into a post-1939-1945 War decline, and now memories alone remain, like the nine wickets for 71 runs taken by Henry Goldstone some 40 plus years ago, in 1959, when Manchester Maccabi were handsomely disposed of in a 62-run win!

Hull Judeans Cricket Club.
Bottom row – 3rd, 4th, 5th from left are: Wass Silverstone, Simon Clyne and Gerry Greenstone, Eric Palmer is 2nd from right on top row. Henry Friedenthal is 6th from the left on top row.

'There is no word in the Hebrew language for "history". Instead of "history" we have "memory". The word occurs no less than 169 times in the Jewish Bible. "History" is his *story, Whereas "memory" is* my *story.'*

Chief Rabbi, 2nd April, 1995.

Jewish Personalities – World Wide

(19th century)

It was during the 19th century that a host of Jewish men of worth, on both the national and the international scene, began the long trail to Jewish respectability in the often hostile environments in which they lived.

Baron Lionel de Rothschild

The year 1858 saw the arrival of political emancipation for the Jews, when Baron Lionel de Rothschild, who, having refused in 1847 to swear an oath of allegiance to Christianity, some eleven years later took an Old Testament oath, and thereby became the first Jew to be returned to the British Parliament.

Benjamin Disraeli

Another turning point in Anglo-Jewish history came in 1881, with the death of Benjamin Disraeli. Prime Minister in 1868 and again from 1874-1880. Although he had been baptised, (a decision by his father, who parted from Judaism) he never ceased to proclaim his sympathy with, and admiration for, the Jewish people. When subjected to a legion of anti-Semitic taunts in the Palace of Westminster, his cutting reply was, 'Yes, I am a Jew, and when the ancestors of the Right Honourable gentleman were brutal savages, mine were priests in the Temple of Solomon.'

Sir Moses Montefiore

The death, in 1885, of Sir Moses Montefiore, at the grand old age of 100, saw the demise of one of the most prominent Jews of the 19th century. One of his many acts of charity came when he met the cost of restoring the Tomb of Rachel, near Bethlehem, in Israel. His death was mourned by the whole nation, regardless of religion or position. A final accolade was a knighthood bestowed on him by Queen Victoria. Montefiore was the inspiration behind the establishment of the first Jewish Quarter to be constructed outside the historic walls of Jerusalem. This area bears the name 'Yemin Moshe'.

Felix Mendelssohn

On the classical music scene, composer Hamburg-born Felix Mendelssohn died, in 1847, at the tragically early age of 38. His music was banned in Germany, due to his Jewish ancestry, in spite of the fact that he had proved to be one of Germany's most famous composers. Mendelssohn's 'Songs without Words' and the Overture to, 'A Midsummer Night's Dream' – the latter composed when he was 16 – are probably the best-known of his compositions.

Baron Von Reuter

The International News Agency was, and possibly still is, dominated by the name Reuter – Baron Von Reuter died in 1899. Beginning as a 'pigeon post' operation, the organisation eventually blossomed into a major news network with its headquarters in London.

Michael Marks

Britain's, if not the world's, best-known retailing trade had its beginnings with Michael Marks, from Russia. Born in 1859, he came to England at 19 years of age, in 1878, and settled (like many other Russian immigrants) in Leeds. In 1884 he worked as a pedlar and, in 1894, he joined with Tom Spencer to found the Marks and Spencer organisation. Michael's premature death, in 1907, temporarily broke the long-standing family connection in management, until four years later, when Michael's son, Simon Marks (later Lord Marks) was elected to the Board, becoming Chairman in 1916. Simon died in 1964. The family connection with well-known names such as Israel Sieff (Simon Mark's brother-in-law) continued the family line. It had been a classic case of Michael's 'penny bazaar' beginnings transforming into a nationally and indeed internationally, well known firm for a century or more.

Baron Lionel de Rothschild.

Benjamin Disraeli

Moses Montefiore

Felix Mendelssohn

Baron Von Reuter

Michael Marks

'Israel will not be judged on its wealth, army or technology, but on its moral image and human values'

David Ben-Gurion

Jewish Personalities – World Wide

(20th Century)

Dr. Theodor Herzl

The 20th century was a mere four years old when the death of the Founder of Zionism, Dr. Theodor Herzl (1860-1904) occurred. Herzl felt strongly that several generations of Jewish 'assimilation' was not an effective way of life for his people, and that only a Jewish State would solve the seemingly timeless Jewish problem of anti-semitism. The impact of the 'Dreyfus affair', in 1894, when Jewish French Army Captain Alfred Dreyfus was falsely convicted of spying for Germany and sentenced to life imprisonment on Devil's island, the French penal colony, (a trial covered by Herzl himself for his newspaper in Vienna) was a further salient factor in Herzl's mission towards the establishment of a World Zionist Movement, in 1897. 'Above all', said Herzl, 'I have come to realise that the solution for us can be found only in Palestine'.

In 1902, during a visit to London, Herzl had provided evidence to the Royal Commission in a plea for a 'legally recognized home in Palestine' for his people. The British Cabinet, in the Balfour Declaration, gave its approval, in 1917, for the 'establishment in Palestine of a national home for the Jewish people . . . it being clearly understood that nothing shall be done which may prejudice the civil and religious rights of existing non-Jewish communities'.

History has shown how those final few words have created the tense Israel-Palestine situation which is still with us some decades later. Soon after the ending of the 1914-1918 War, the League of Nations gave Britain a Mandate to administer Palestine and, indeed, the first High Commissioner, Sir Herbert Samuel was Jewish.

On Herzl's premature death, in 1904, his fervent wish to be re-interred in Israel (a wish signified in his will) was eventually granted by the Knesset (Israeli Parliament) in 1949.

David Ben Gurion

David Ben Gurion, born in Plonsk, Poland, moved to Palestine, in 1906, as a 20-year-old, and proved to be a leading figure with the Zionist movement. He was no friend of the British during the Mandate period, especially rebelling against the policy of limited immigration of Jews from the horrors of Europe at the end of World War II.

He led the Jewish Agency and the 'illegal' (depending on which side of the political fence you were) Hagganah; became Israel's first Prime Minister, serving from 1948 to 1953 and also from 1955 to 1963, and, in similar vein to Herzl, declared that all Jews should return to Israel as the National Home and a place of safety. Ben Gurion died in 1973, at the age of 87, having retired to Kibbutz Sder Boker, in the Negev, now a memorial to his achievements.

Chaim Weizmann

Israel's first State President, (elected in May 1948), Chaim Weizmann, was also a dedicated Zionist. Born near Pinsk, in Russia, now Belarus, he studied in Berlin and, in 1904, came to England to work in the chemicals industry. His overtures to the British hierarchy to allow immigration to Israel of displaced Jews from Europe fell on deaf ears, but U.S. President Harry Truman came to Weizmann's aid by securing American recognition of Israel in May 1948, when statehood was declared. Weizmann died in 1952 and the Weizmann Institute in Rehovot is dedicated to his memory.

Golda Meir

One of the world's first women Prime Ministers, Israeli leader Golda Meir (1898-1978) became an international figure. Born in Kiev, Russia, she emigrated with her family to the U.S.A. as a child of eight, in 1906. She became an ardent Zionist, which naturally attracted her to Israel, where she became the country's Prime Minister in 1969. Her autobiography 'My Life' was internationally acclaimed.

Moshe Dayan

Not surprisingly, in a country such as Israel, where war has almost been a way of life (and death), military heroes have always been in abundant supply, but few with such a magical personality as Moshe Dayan. The loss of one eye (in the British military action against the Vichy, Pro-Nazi, regime in Syria) was hidden by a distinctive eye-patch, a 'trademark' which became well known virtually world-wide.

He was born on the first kibbutz, Deganya, in 1915, and the army dominated his life. Having trained under British Captain Orde Wingate, who himself trained Jewish commandos against the Arab enemy, Dayan's speedy promotion saw him as Chief of Staff of the Israeli Army, and his subsequent victories were in the Suez War of 1956 and in the 1967 Six Day War, as recently appointed Minister of Defence. He died in October 1981, probably the most respected war hero of the fledgling state. (Photograph page 25).

Emanuel Shinwell

On the *British* political scene, Emanuel Shinwell, known affectionately as 'Manny', was probably the best known British politician, Jewish or otherwise, outside of the Prime Minister, for most of the 20th century. Born in London's East End, in 1884, he and his family moved to Glasgow when he was a child, and, in consequence, he acquired a pronounced Scottish accent which led people to assume, wrongly, that he was a Scot by birth. A succession of Labour Government positions, including Minister of Defence, Minister of Fuel and Power, and Secretary of State for War, put 'Manny' (later Lord Shinwell) in the forefront of Labour politics virtually until his death in 1986, at the age of 102!

Abba Eban

Born in Cape Town, South Africa, in 1915, *The man with the golden tongue* is an apt soubriquet for a prominent Israeli diplomat and politician. By name Abba Eban, his disciplines, during his University of Cambridge days, were in the field of languages, principally related to the Middle East.

He served as Israel's representative at the United Nations from Israel's formal acceptance as a State. After his appointment as Israeli ambassador to the U.S.A. he returned to Israel, and joined the Israeli Cabinet, becoming Deputy Prime Minister and in 1966, Foreign Minister.

His work in the media has given him the right to the claim of the political voice of Israel, by virtue of his authorship of books such as 'My People' and writing and presentation of a host of television documentaries.

Rabbi Jakobovits

A unique Rabbinic figure of the 20th century was British Chief Rabbi Immanuel Jakobovits, who sadly died, at 78 years of age, just two months before the opening of the new Millennium. He held the position from 1967-1991, and was the first Chief Rabbi to be knighted in Office, and, in 1988, became the first to sit in the House of Lords, a distinction applauded not only by Jewish sources, but by leading representatives of all Britain's *Christian* Churches.

Born in Konigsberg, East Prussia, in 1921, his family fled from Berlin and moved to England

at the time of the rise of Hitler.

His initial Rabbinate was in London after which, at only 27 years of age, he became Chief Rabbi of Ireland, followed by the position of Rabbi of New York's 5th Avenue Synagogue, before returning to Britain in 1967.

Lord Jakobovits left behind six children and more than 30 grandchildren.

The present Chief Rabbi, Dr. Jonathan Sacks, described his predecessor as 'the outstanding Rabbinic figure of his generation'. Rabbi Jakobovits, a President of the Council of Christians and Jews was a national spokesman on the subjects of Jewish dietary laws and Israeli foreign policy – feeling strongly that *traditional Judaism needed no amending to meet current trends.* He was buried in Jerusalem in late October 1999.

Albert Einstein

So we turn to science, in which Albert Einstein (1879-1955) was a 'giant' in his field. His Theory of Relativity, while not readily understood by the layman, proved a turning point in scientific history. His efforts were rewarded with the Nobel Prize for Physics in 1921.

Born of Jewish parents at Ulm, in Germany, he eventually made his home in America to escape the Hitler regime in 1933. In November 1952, Israeli Prime Minister David Ben Gurion offered Einstein the Presidency of the State. Einstein wrote 'I lack both the natural aptitude and the experience to deal with people . . . but am deeply moved by the offer from our State of Israel and at once saddened and ashamed that I cannot accept.'

School pupils who read this book, after suffering a poor school report, should take consolation, since young Albert Einstein was dismissed academically by his teachers as a 'no-hoper'.

Leonard Bernstein

The Jewish world of music produced contrasting notable figures. The magical songs of *West Side Story,* will always be associated with Leonard Bernstein (1918-1990), as the television programme which featured the 'Master' in rehearsal, proved. In addition, his extensive repertoire included both classical music and jazz. His long-standing relationship, as conductor of the New York Philharmonic, lasted over 30 years from 1958 to his death.

Dame Marie Rambert

Pioneer of British ballet, Dame Marie Rambert founded the ballet Rambert. Born in Warsaw, Poland, in 1888, she was still inspiring her pupils virtually until her death some 94 years later, in 1982. Recognition of Dame Marie's talent came in 1954 with the award of the C.B.E. and the French Legion of Honour, in 1957. The ultimate accolade of being made a Dame came in 1962.

Jacqueline du Pré

Brilliant cellist Jacqueline du Pré, who tragically died of multiple sclerosis in 1987, at only 42 years of age, had converted to Judaism on marrying Israeli pianist and conductor Daniel Barenboim, in 1967. Her physical and mental courage in fighting her life-threatening illness, while continuing her public appearances and master classes, was an inspiration to her world-wide devotees. She received an O.B.E. in 1976.

Barbra Streisand

Controversially, perhaps, should be added the 'Funny Girl' herself, Barbra Streisand, who, in spite of the incentive of cosmetic surgery in acquiring the 'film star' look, kept her Jewish features intact, and turned them to total advantage, as a host of film awards and gold and platinum albums prove. Born Brooklyn, New York, in 1942, she now owns her own film company, and like film director Steven Spielberg, of *Shindler's List* fame – another world-wide Jewish personality – is producing television and film material featuring tributes to both Holocaust victims and survivors.

Her films have massive appeal due – in part – to the Jewish-American style portrayal of the characters she plays. Within three years (1968-70) came an Oscar-winning performance as best Actress, in *Funny Girl*; the memorable *Hello Dolly* (a 'must' for amateur dramatic companies, world-wide); and *On A Clear Day You Can See For Ever.*

She took up the producer's reins with the film *Yentl* which required a considerable leap of imagination, as a young Jewish girl attends a male seminary (Yeshiva) and remains unrecognised! Not a great success but it epitomised Barbra's energy and creativity.

Her effigy in the Jewish American Hall of Fame Museum alongside such 'greats' as Albert Einstein, Golda Meir and George Gershwin is the ultimate recognition of her multiple talents.

George Gershwin

Born Jacob Gershwine in September 1898, in Brooklyn, New York, George Gershwin, who died in 1937, a few months before his 39th birthday, will forever be linked with *Embraceable You, A Foggy Day, Rhapsody in Blue* and *Porgy and Bess*. He was, in short, the foremost composer of some of the most popular music of the 20th century.

Yehudi Menuhin

Born in New York in 1916, Yehudi Menuhin became one of the great musical geniuses of the 20th century by virtue of his superlative violin playing. He was equally adept at orchestral conducting and, as a teacher of music, inspired young violinists to achieve the musical heights of the 'Master'. While on tour in March 1999, Lord Menuhin died of a heart attack at 82 years of age, causing world-wide grief among his millions of admirers.

In 1993, he was made Lord Menuhin of Stoke D'Abernon, named after the venue for his school for gifted – but less well off – young musicians. His coat of arms included, inevitably, a violin string, but also a menorah, the eight-branched candelabra used at the Feast of Lights, namely the Festival of Chanukah, and as a representation of the State of Israel. (In the grounds of the Knesset, the Israeli Parliament, in Jerusalem, can be seen an impressive menorah presented by the British Parliament.)

Sigmund Freud

Psycho-analyst Sigmund Freud's originality of thought dominated the world headlines. A professor of neurology in Vienna, he fled the Nazi threat and died in London at the outbreak of the 1939-45 War.

Lord Joseph Duveen

'Local boy' to Hull, English art dealer Lord Joseph Duveen, was born in the city in October 1869, and later moved to London. He was knighted in 1919, created a baronet in 1927, a baron in 1938, and built the new wing of the Tate Gallery in London which bears his name. Later, he added a gallery to the British Museum to display the Elgin Marbles. His father had come to Hull from Holland, in 1867 and transformed his family salesman's business into a highly successful enterprise. Lord Joseph died in London in May 1939.

Marc Chagall

Artist Marc Chagall left Russia in 1922, at 35 years of age, and made his reputation as a leading surrealist painter. His stained glass windows, featuring the Twelve Tribes of Israel, can be seen in the Hadassah Medical Centre in Jerusalem. Uniquely, he created the first Jewish artist's work to be commissioned by the Vatican. He died in Saint-Paul, France, two years, or so, short of his 100th birthday.

Jacob Epstein

The great sculptor Jacob Epstein had fame initially thrust upon him due to his controversial works of naked and explicit human figures. His religious output included sculptures of Adam and Jacob. He died in 1959, having received a K.B.E. in 1954.

Mark Spitz

In sport, outstanding American swimmer Mark Spitz, born in 1950, won a record seven gold medals at the Munich Olympic Games in 1972. These were for the 100 and 200 metres freestyle and butterfly, the 4 x 100 and 4 x 200 metres freestyle relays, and the 4 x 100 metres medley relay. This was a record number of gold medals gained at a single Olympics.

The following necessarily restricted list includes 20th century Nobel Prize winners: Boris Pasternak (Literature, 1958); Henry Kissinger (Peace, 1973); Isaac Bashevis Singer (Literature, 1978); Menachem Begin (Peace, 1978); Yitzhak Rabin (Peace) and Shimon Peres (Peace 1994), the final trio becoming Prime Ministers of Israel.

Anne Frank

Finally, an unforgettable 20th-century name, which, above all, appeals to the emotions of *all* age-groups, is that of a Jewish teenage girl.

Among more than a million Jewish children killed in the Holocaust, Dutch girl Anne Frank displayed her astonishing literary ability, even under the mental pressure of hiding from the Nazi threat with her family in a house in Amsterdam.

She wrote what has since been acknowledged as a definitive document of life at as teenage girl under Nazi occupation. Anne died in Bergen-Belsen Concentration Camp in March 1945, at 16 years of age. Her Diary has since been translated into 55 languages and has sold more than 25 million copies. The house in which the Frank family lived has become a museum visited by people of all nationalities – more than 800,000 in 1998.

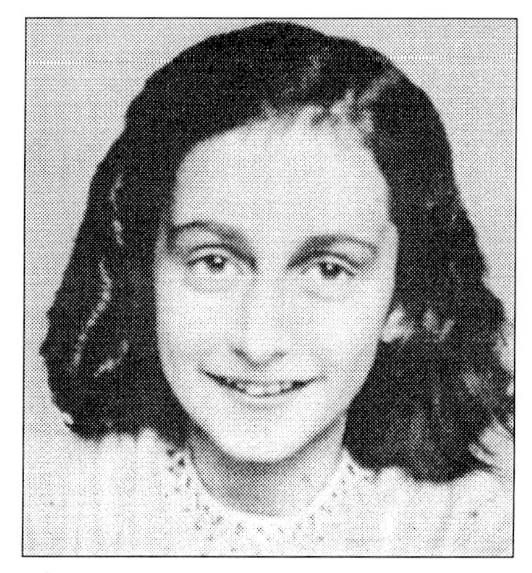

One of the plaques in the 'Hull Hebrew Synagogue', adjoining the Memorial Window for the Six Million, and has Anne Frank's name attached, fittingly ends this 20th-century list. It reads:

> 'Who knows, it might even be our religion from which the world and all the peoples learn good, and for that reason and that reason only do we have to suffer now!'
>
> Anne Frank

FOOTNOTES

1. Video entitled *The History of Hull's Orthodox Synagogues, 1780-1995.*
2. Usury was condemned by the Church and the King, decreeing it to be immoral to loan money at interest. Such was the hypocrisy of this view that, when Christian agencies were set up offering the same services, the system became totally acceptable.
3. A further 'coincidence' was the expulsion of Spanish Jewry on the 9th of Av, 1492, by the Spanish monarchs, Ferdinand and Isabella.
4. B.C.E. – Before the Common (Christian) Era; C.E. – In the Common (Christian) Era.
5. Figures vary from the 15,000 quoted to far fewer, due to the many (especially the more affluent Jews) who had already left these shores.
6. Spanish word for 'pigs' or 'swine'.
7. The visit of Princess Anne, daughter of King James II, to a Sephardic Synagogue in London in 1685, during the Festival of Passover – the first visit to a Synagogue of a future monarch – was probably a landmark in the acceptance of the Jewish role in English society.
8. Posterngate was one of Hull's entrance gates in its medieval wall. Posterngate, now a street, runs between the relatively newly constructed Princes Quay complex and Hull's Market Place. The only remaining gateway of the original entrances into Hull's Old Town is the Beverley Gate, in the present Hull's principal shopping area. Its long-standing fame relates to its closure against Charles I, in 1642, prior to the outbreak of the Civil War.
9. The demonstration was eventually put down by the Army.
10. A 'minyan' is the term for the minimum number of Jewish men who need to be present for communal prayer – the traditional number is ten or more.
11. Yiddish originated among German Jews in the Middle Ages – an amalgam of words from a variety of countries – spoken mainly by Central European Jewry.
12. The assassination, in 1881, of Tsar Alexander II, by revolutionaries, in Russia, created officially organised pogroms by the Russian Government in an attempt to deflect their unpopularity on to the Jewish minority, a well-used formula then, and since. Many deaths and large-scale destruction of Jewish property took place and mass emigration resulted in over three million Jews leaving in the 33-year period up to the outbreak of the 1914-18 War.

    A majority travelled to the U.S.A. and Western Europe, in excess of 100,000 came, and remained, in Britain.

    The menace of Hitlerite Germany further swelled the British-Jewish immigration figures in the 1930s to in excess of a quarter of a million by the 1950s.
13. The Wilberforce Council was named after Hull-born William Wilberforce, who led the campaign for the abolition of slavery in the British Empire. The Council existed to keep in written contact with Russian Jews and assist their exodus from the oppressive regime in which they lived.
14. Linnaeus Street, the location of Hull's first Botanic Gardens, was named after the well-known Swedish botanist, Carl Linnaeus, famous for his work in plant classification.
15. B. S. Jacobs designed several important structures both at home and abroad, including the Hudson Bridge in Canada.
16. Henry Feldman's four-year tenure of office as Hull's Mayor has only once been surpassed, when William Alfred Gelder served for five years from 1898 to 1904.
17. The 'Torah' is the name given to the five books of Moses, written in Hebrew on a scroll and recited during Synagogue services. Appropriate extracts are usually sung by the cantor rather than simply read.
18. Currently such funeral arrangements are ably continued by Barry Schneider, Alf Klarik, and dedicated helpers.
19. 'Shammas' is the Hebrew equivalent of Beadle.
20. 'Beth Hamedrash' (House of Study) – there is little distinction between a 'Beth Hamedrash' and a Synagogue, except the assumption that a synagogue is the larger of the two buildings.
21. Ninety per cent of Hull property was either damaged or destroyed during the 1939-45 War.
22. In similar vein to Conrad Segelman at the Hull Western.
23. The late Maurice Lipman was the father of well-known Hull actress Maureen Lipman, who was awarded an Honorary Degree by Hull University.
24. The Israeli National Council met in the Tel Aviv Museum to hear Prime Minister David Ben Gurion announce Israel's Declaration of Independence, incorporating an 'open door' policy on Jewish immigration; freedom of religion; and equality of social and political rights 'irrespective of religion, race or sex'.
25. The Pryme Street Synagogue had been operative for about a year prior to its formal opening.
26. Some 170 years earlier, in 1826, a similar amalgamation of 'Posterngate' and 'Parade Row' had taken place.
27. A 'yeshiva' is a Jewish school of learning to attain religious qualifications.
28. This common formula is, of course, at variance with the existing Anglican and Roman Catholic schools, where religious education can range from a short act of daily religious worship (compulsory by law in an otherwise secular environment), to schools with a religious foundation, where the school ethos relates all school work to the specific religion concerned.
29. Rabbi E. S. Rabinowitz, B.A. was inducted as the first *communal* rabbi of Hull by Chief Rabbi Israel Brodie, in August, 1956.
30. The word 'seder' is Hebrew for 'Order of Service' at a special commemorative meal which is served, at home, to family and friends on the first two nights of the eight-day Passover Festival.
31. The Haggadah is a book, in Hebrew and English, containing the story of the Children of Israel's years of slavery under their Egyptian task-masters. The father reads the narrative at the Seder service. 'Why,' asks the youngest child, 'is this night *different* from all other nights?' A perfect cue for father to respond by using the Haggadah, which contains Biblical extracts, prayers and light-hearted songs, to hold the interest – especially that of the children – during a somewhat protracted service.

INDEX (except Appendices)

Final Quotes

'My relationship to the Jewish people has become my strongest human bond ever since I became fully aware of our precarious situation among the nations of the world'.

Albert Einstein (1879-1955).

'The source of Jewish life is not within the synagogue but within us'.

Rabbi Shalom Osdoba at his induction ceremony, Hull Hebrew Synagogue, April 1995.

'Grandfather, you were and still are, our hero. I want you to know that in all I have ever done, I have always seen you before my eyes. Your esteem and love accompanied us on every step, and on every path, and we lived in the light of your values'.

Eulogy by Noa Ben-Artzi, grand-daughter of assassinated Israeli Prime Minister Yitzak Rabin (1995) at his funeral.

The warmth of a Jewish community is in inverse proportion to its size. You don't *count* Jews, you make certain that every Jew *counts*'.

Chief Rabbi. Dr. Jonathan Sacks, at opening Hull Hebrew Synagogue, April 1995.

'Will-power alone saw me through'.

Hull Jewish soldier, Leslie Kersh, on his release after 3½ years as Japanese prisoner-of-war, in Changi Jail, in Singapore.

'Traditional Judaism needs *no amending* to meet current trends.'

Late Chief Rabbi, Immanuel Jakobovits. (1921-1999).

INVITATION TO PURCHASE THE VIDEO ENTITLED

THE HISTORY OF HULL'S ORTHODOX SYNAGOGUES

1780-1995

Over 18 months in the making, produced by Elliot Oppel, M.A., B.Sc. Cert Educ. in collaboration with the Audio Visual Department of the University of Hull, with a duration of 70 minutes, the Video is in two parts:

Part One (53 minutes) covers the history of the Jewish peoples in this country: their earliest arrival in the reign of William the Conqueror; their 'Expulsion' by Edward I in 1290; the 'Return' in Oliver Cromwell's day; the mere handful of Jewish immigrants who came to Hull in the late 18th century; the influx of Jewish immigrants to Hull from the pogroms of Eastern Europe in the early 1900s.

This provides the essential historical background material as Hull's Synagogues – from Posterngate, in 1780, to Pryme Street, in 1995 – via Parade Row, Robinson Row, the Hull Western, the Hull Old Hebrew, the Central, Lower Union Street etc. – are featured, together with interviews with local personalities from the Jewish community, past and present.

Part Two (17 minutes) concentrates on the formal opening of the Hull Hebrew Congregation Synagogue, on 2 April, 1995, by the Chief Rabbi, Dr. Jonathan Sacks, the induction of Rabbi S. Osdoba, and the children's involvement.

If interested in purchasing one or more Videos, by cheque at £17.99 each, made out to Elliot Oppel, please be kind enough to send to: 'Highgate of Beverley', 4 Newbegin, Beverley, East Yorkshire, HU17 8AP, enclosing your cheque, name and home address, and the number of Videos required.

Videos will be personally delivered to your home address if in the Hull area, or otherwise sent by post.

NATIONAL COMMENTS received: *Informative - enjoyable - totally professional,* Ruth Pringle, Cranbrook, Kent. *Interesting to see how the history of the Hull community has evolved over the decades,* Howard Foreman, General Manager, 'All Abroad', Leeds. *Superb effort!* Jackie Kalms, Shoeburyness, Essex. *Result of massive research brings you credit.* Bernard Levy, Oxon. *Congratulations on a magnificent effort,* Darryl Mydat, Ilford, Essex, plus congratulatory messages from both Church and Synagogue clergy.